15-20

Charlotte Perkins Gilman

Twayne's United States Authors Series

David J. Nordloh, Editor

Indiana University, Bloomington

TUSAS 482

CHARLOTTE PERKINS GILMAN
(1860–1935)
Courtesy of Schlesinger Library,
Radcliffe College

Charlotte Perkins Gilman

By Gary Scharnhorst

University of Texas at Dallas

Twayne Publishers • Boston

Charlotte Perkins Gilman

Gary Scharnhorst

Copyright © 1985 by G.K. Hall & Company
All Rights Reserved
Published by Twayne Publishers
A Division of G. K. Hall & Co.
A publishing subsidiary of ITT
70 Lincoln Street
Boston, Massachusetts 02111

Book Production by Marne B. Sultz
Book Design by Barbara Anderson

Printed on permanent/durable acid-free
paper and bound in the United States of
America.

Library of Congress Cataloging in Publication Data

Scharnhorst, Gary.
    Charlotte Perkins Gilman.

    (Twayne's United States authors series; TUSAS 482)
    Bibliography: p. 134
    Includes index.

    1. Gilman, Charlotte Perkins, 1860–1935—
Criticism and interpretation.
I. Title. II. Series.
PS1744.G57Z85 1985   828'.409   84-19208
ISBN 0-8057-7435-1

To my daughter Emily,
in anticipation of a better day

Contents

About the Author

Gary Scharnhorst holds the Ph.D. in American studies from Purdue University. During 1978–79 he served as a Fulbright lecturer at Stuttgart University in West Germany, and he now teaches in the School of Arts and Humanities at the University of Texas at Dallas. He has contributed essays to such journals as *American Quarterly*, *American Literature, American Literary Realism, American Transcendentalist Quarterly*, and *Studies in Short Fiction*. He also has written the monograph on Horatio Alger, Jr., in Twayne's United States Authors Series.

Preface

"One of the great women of the [past] two centuries," the novelist Zona Gale called her at her death in 1935.[1] Though Charlotte Perkins Gilman is best known today as the author of *Women and Economics* (1898), a pioneering study of the "economic factor between men and women as a factor in social evolution," she was first acclaimed by nineteenth-century readers as a poet and writer of realistic fiction depicting the plight of women. Her first book, in fact, was a collection of verse entitled *In This Our World* (1893). W. D. Howells, the dean of American letters, was profoundly impressed by "The Yellow Wallpaper" (1892), her celebrated story of mental breakdown. Over the past decade it has been increasingly anthologized for general readers. Throughout her prolific career, especially while publisher and sole author of the *Forerunner* (1909–16), Gilman composed didactic poetry and fiction that complemented her nonfiction. In all, she wrote three utopian romances, five novels, barrels of uncollected articles, poems, and short stories that appeared in both scholarly and popular periodicals, an autobiography, an unpublished detective story, as well as a collection of verse and six books of essays. During the seven years she wrote the *Forerunner* alone, according to her own estimate, she produced the equivalent of twenty-eight books at the rate of 21,000 words per month.[2] All of her major works, including the full seven volumes of the *Forerunner,* have been reprinted within the past few years. Yet there remains no thorough study of her imaginative work as a whole, no attempt to relate her poetry and fiction to her essays.

Thus in this monograph I will focus on Gilman as a litterateur. The scope of previous scholarship has been largely limited to her theoretical writings or her private life. When discussed at all, her fiction, especially "The Yellow Wall-paper," has usually been deemed thinly disguised memoir. Her poetry has been virtually ignored. However, because the whole of her canon shares the same didactic purpose, it seems reasonable to consider her verse, fiction, and nonfiction as complementary bodies of literature. "In my opinion," she once declared, "it is a pretty poor thing to write, to talk, without a purpose" (*L,* 121). To be sure, her didacticism may be most explicit in her essays, but it is both foreshadowed and amplified in her poetry and fiction. Moreover, though she often disclaimed any literary pretensions, Gilman wrote her essays to express ideas "with clearness and vivacity" so that they "might be apprehended with ease and pleasure" (*L*, 284–85). Her treatises were often praised for wit and clarity of style.

Like her fellow New Englander and contemporary Henry Adams, Charlotte Perkins Gilman defies simple categorization. Her work transcends the superficial distinctions among scholarly disciplines and, like a rich legacy bequested to several heirs, it belongs in common to the literary critic, the social scientist, and the intellectual historian. For that reason, I have chosen to discuss Gilman's oeuvre chronologically and thematically rather than opt for a genre-based study. Each of the five chapters is devoted to a period of Gilman's life with particular reference to the work she produced during that period. I have attempted to write, in short, a type of literary biography, a review and analysis of her career as an author and lecturer. Readers interested in a more intimate portrait of Gilman should consult one of the works by Mary A. Hill or Carol Berkin listed in the Selected Bibliography.

In my opinion, the key to Gilman's thought, the most pronounced theme in her work, is her perfectionism. She was a latter-day utopian, no less. She occasionally deprecated the term "feminist,"[3] which often connoted "suffragist," believing it too narrow to encompass the range of her social criticism. "My business was to find out what ailed society, and how most easily and naturally to improve it," as she wrote in her autobiography (*L*, 182). She was an early advocate of Edward Bellamy's utopian schemes, a Nationalist lecturer, and some of her earliest work was contributed to the magazines of the Bellamy clubs. Her later work, including *Women and Economics* and *Herland* (1915), elaborates on and extends the tenets of socialism and reform Darwinism. Late in her career, in such essays as "Making Towns Fit to Live In" (1921), she turned her attention to the problems of the modern city. Her suggested reforms, such as centralizing food, laundry, and heating services and zoning land to maximize open space, once more echoed Bellamy's *Looking Backward*. In short, Gilman loosed a lively and catholic imagination upon a variety of social problems and envisioned a thorough social reformation. As she once concluded, "This is the woman's century, the first chance for the mother of the world to rise to her full place, her transcendent power to remake humanity, to rebuild the suffering world" (*L,* 331). To her credit, Gilman never lost faith that, when the female half of humanity is fully enfranchised, politically and especially economically, the man-made world will be fundamentally reformed. If her millennial optimism seems misplaced to us now, more is the pity: to that extent may we measure our own loss of faith.

A note on names: the subject of this monograph was named Charlotte Anna Perkins from her birth in 1860 until her marriage in 1884, Charlotte Perkins Stetson until her second marriage in 1900, and Charlotte Perkins Gilman until her death in 1935. At the risk of confusing the reader, I identify her in this work by all three names, depending upon the period under discussion. The only single-name alternatives were "Charlotte," which seemed too smug and familiar, and "Gilman," a name by which she was not known until the age of forty. "It would have saved trouble had I remained Perkins from the first," as she allowed in her autobiography, for "this changing of women's names is a nuisance we are now happily outgrowing (*L,* 284).

I wish to thank Nancy Tuana and Mary-Margaret Byerman for patient criticism of my manuscript, though I claim full responsibility, for better or worse, for the contents of this volume. Cole Dawson, Jack Bales, and Shannon Bailey helped me to compile a bibliography of Gilman's works. I wish also to acknowledge the assistance of the staff of the Schlesinger Library at Radcliffe College, depository of the Charlotte Perkins Gilman Papers, for prompt replies to my frequent requests for material. This project was also supported in part by an Organized Research Grant, which I received from the University of Texas at Dallas. Part of chapter one has appeared in different form in *California History*.

Gary Scharnhorst

University of Texas at Dallas

Chronology

1860 Charlotte Anna Perkins born 3 July in Hartford, Connecticut, to Frederick Beecher Perkins and Mary Westcott Perkins.

1869 Parents permanently separate.

1878–1879 Attends the Rhode Island School of Design.

1884 January, publishes first poem, "In Duty Bound," in *Woman's Journal*. 2 May, marries artist Charles Walter Stetson.

1885 23 March, daughter Katharine Beecher Stetson born.

1886 Treated for "hysteria" by the nerve specialist S. Weir Mitchell.

1888 Separated from Stetson. Moves to Pasadena, California.

1890 April, poem "Similar Cases" published in the *Nationalist*.

1890–1894 Active in the Nationalist movement in California.

1891 Moves to Oakland and joins the Pacific Coast Women's Press Association.

1892 January, story "The Yellow Wall-paper" published in the *New England Magazine*.

1893 *In This Our World*, a collection of verse, her first book.

1894 April, divorced from Stetson. Moves to San Francisco to edit the *Impress*.

1895 Second edition of *In This Our World*.

1896 January, meets Lester Frank Ward at Women's Suffrage Convention in Washington, D.C. July, attends the International Socialist and Labor Congress in London.

1898 *Women and Economics;* third, enlarged edition of *In This Our World*.

1899 Attends the International Women's Congress in London.

1900 11 June, marries George Houghton Gilman and settles in New York. *Concerning Children*.

1903   *The Home: Its Work and Influence.*

1904   Attends the International Congress of Women in Berlin. *Human Work.*

1905   Lecture tour of England, Holland, Germany, Austria, and Hungary.

1907   *Women and Social Service.*

1909–1916   Single-handedly edits and publishes monthly magazine the *Forerunner.*

1910   *What Diantha Did,* a novel.

1911   *The Man-Made World; The Crux* and *Moving the Mountain,* novels.

1913   Attends the International Woman's Suffrage Congress in Budapest.

1915   *Herland* serialized in the *Forerunner.*

1919   Contributes articles to the *New York Tribune* syndicate.

1920–1921   Publishes essays on urban planning.

1922   Moves to Norwich Town, Connecticut.

1923   *His Religion and Hers.*

1927   December, "Progress Through Birth Control" published in the *North American Review.*

1934   May, moves to Pasadena, near her daughter Katharine, after death of her husband.

1935   17 August, Gilman dies in Pasadena. October, *The Living of Charlotte Perkins Gilman,* an autobiography, published posthumously.

Chapter One
The Early Years

On 28 July 1930, a few days after celebrating her seventieth birthday, Charlotte Perkins Gilman complained to the psychologist Samuel D. Schmalhausen that "in my judgement 'the woman question' has hardly been asked, much less answered. We have had the struggle for 'rights' and all this uproar about sex, but hardly any study of the biologic and sociologic effects of the aborted development of half the race."[1] After a forty-year campaign for reform, Gilman was not conceding defeat but sounding her most characteristic note. Her social convictions and reform impulse were rooted in her earliest experiences. As Mary A. Hill has observed, "Charlotte was born into a family for whom conventional sex-role expectations didn't fit."[2]

Beginnings

On the eve of Independence Day in 1860, Charlotte Anna Perkins was born in Hartford, Connecticut, into the family Beecher. She was a rebel by birthright. Her father, Frederick Beecher Perkins, was the nephew of Harriet Beecher Stowe and Henry Ward Beecher, earnest evangelicals who aspired to save the world, if not refashion it in their own image; Catharine Beecher, founder of the Hartford Female Seminary and proponent of "domestic feminism"; as well as Isabella Beecher Hooker, an eccentric suffragist who expected to be anointed matriarch of the American nation when women at last received the vote. Frederick Perkins was also the brother-in-law of Edward Everett Hale, a liberal Unitarian minister and man of letters, author in 1863 of "The Man Without a Country." In 1857, Frederick Perkins had married his distant cousin Mary Fitch Wescott of Providence, Rhode Island, a descendant of one of Roger Williams's dissenting deacons. They had three children in the space of three years. After a fourth child died in infancy in 1866, as Charlotte noted in her autobiography, "The doctor said if my mother had another baby she would die. Presently my father left home. Whether the doctor's dictum was the reason or merely a reason I do not know. What I do know is that my

I

childhood had no father" (L, 5). Nor did Frederick Perkins assume
financial responsibility for the family who, like nomads, moved eigh-
teen times over the next fourteen years. Frederick and Mary Perkins
divorced in 1873. Their daughter learned early to question the sanc-
tity of the home, the "domestic mythology," and the role assigned to
women within the conjugal family. In later years, Frederick Perkins
worked as a librarian in Boston and San Francisco, and also served as
the librarian of the Bohemian Club in California.

By all accounts Charlotte Perkins was a precocious child. Before
the age of five, she had taught herself to read, whetting her taste for
literature with such pabulum as Hooker's *Child's Book of Nature* and
issues of *Our Young Folks,* the juvenile version of the *Atlantic Monthly.*
Her occasional childhood visits to the home of Harriet Stowe in Hartford were especially memorable: "Aunt Harriet used to sit at a small
table in that back parlor, looking out on the flowers and ferns and
little fountain while she painted in water colors," she later recalled
(L, 16). Harriet Beecher Stowe, more than any other woman Charlotte Perkins knew as a child, served as her role model. She thought
her aunt "one of the world's greatest women" who led a life "perfect
in the fulfillment of all daily service, of all intimate personal relations, and yet fulfilling also the public claim of service to
humanity."[3] She aspired to the same goals, with decidedly mixed
success.

At the age of eight, like most children, Charlotte Perkins exercised
a vivid imagination. Every night, she later reminisced, "I would
think only of pleasant things that really might happen; once a week
I would think of lovelier, stranger things, once a month of wonders,
and once a year of anything I wanted to!" She was particularly impressed by *Oliver Twist* and soon invented a fantastic realm where,
like Dickens's hero, she reigned as a princess in disguise. For five
years, she savored her reveries, even wrote elaborate fairy tales, many
still extant, about a princess with magical powers who subdues the
forces of evil or conveys unhappy children to a South Seas paradise.
After five years, alarmed by "what she was led to suppose this inner
light might become," her mother commanded her "to give it up."
She obeyed, though she well understood the sacrifice: "Night after
night to shut the door on happiness, and hold it shut. Never, when
dear, bright, glittering dreams pushed hard, to let them in" (L, 20–
24). The episode might serve as a paradigm of her later life and work:
she would war against oppression no less than her fanciful princess.

She would conceive ideal worlds and lead her readers to them. She would beware of personal pleasure and intimacy to prove the measure of her self-discipline. And she would repress her imaginative and fanciful faculties, as if she mistrusted them, to pay allegiance to empirical science.

Even in adolescence, by her own admission, she was willful and headstrong. "A strong-minded woman I will be if I have to wade in blood as the ancient bravado have it," as she wrote a friend, Martha Luther.[4] One of the major events of her life, she explained in her autobiography, occurred when, at the age of fifteen, she defied another of her mother's commands—on this occasion, to apologize for an offense she did not commit. The refusal was tantamount to a personal declaration of independence from the Victorian "cult of true womanhood." She discovered that "One could suffer, one could die if it came to that, but one could not be coerced. I was born . . ." (*L*, 34). With a heady sense of freedom, she commenced an ambitious program of self-culture. Her formal education to date had been limited to four years of public and private schools. She began to "read voraciously." Among the works that impressed her most were James Freeman Clarke's *Ten Great Religions,* Emerson's *Essays,* Scott's romances, Dickens's novels. In her diary, she also confessed to an affection for popular sentimental fiction, such as the stories of Louisa May Alcott and Mrs. A. D. T. Whitney, at which she and her mother would "weep and snivel consumedly."[5] At the age of seventeen, she wrote her long-absent father, the author of *The Best Reading,* to ask him to suggest books for her, and he replied with a list of histories and popular studies in ethnology, anthropology, and evolutionary science, including Andrew White's *Warfare of Religion and Science* (1876). "I now read connectedly," she later recalled, "learning the things I most wanted to know, in due order and sequence, none of them exhaustedly but all in due relation" (*L*, 37). Over the years, moreover, she formed friendships with the families of Frederic Henry Hedge, one of the founders of the old Transcendentalist Club in Boston, and William F. Channing, son of William Ellery Channing. She relished their "broad free-thinking, scientific talk, earnest promotion of great causes" (*L*, 49). And in 1880, at the age of twenty, she completed a two-year course of study at the Rhode Island School of Design.

Increasingly, she had discovered a world "suffering from many needless evils," in particular "the injustices under which women suffered" (*L*, 61). Like a scientist testing through trial and error, she had formulated a personal creed akin to Unitarianism, conceiving of God not as a "heavenly father" or transcendent patriarch but a rational power or immanent presence. "This religion of mine underlies all my Living," she later wrote (L, 39). Her theology of works was predicated upon the notion that the "first duty of a human being is to assume right functional relation to society" (L, 42). She once attended a "meeting of some earnest temperance workers," for example, "but was not at home in that atmosphere of orthodox religion and strong emotion" (L, 61). Similarly, she was largely unmoved by the suffrage movement. "I never was a very ardent suffragist," she confided to a friend in 1890. "It has long seemed such a foregone conclusion that I can't get at all excited about it."[6] Unfortunately, in her opinion, popular campaigns to ameliorate the plight of women merely treated symptoms, not the sources of social malaise. The vote per se was no panacea for economic inequality between the sexes. Her incipient feminism was, for better or worse, largely intellectual.

At twenty-one, she aspired not to a career in public service or political association, but to a literary and artistic life. "I realize[d] more & more how much I depend on outside influences, whether books, people, or active surroundings," she wrote Martha Luther after a particularly boring afternoon in 1881, "and flew to Emerson. . . . And O Martha, just look here! *I was right,* I read Emerson's incomprehensible conundrums! My mind was his for a moment!"[7] A week later, she declared her intention "to keep up with the literature and art of the day" and, after another week, announced that "I think G. Eliot will be very much to me."[8] She was earning a modest living as a freelance commercial artist and private teacher, and she was a poet by avocation. She had embarked on a program of exercise and physical culture, and she refused to wear corsets or dress according to the dictates of feminine fashion. Her closest friend was a young woman in whose company she realized "my first deep personal happiness" (L, 48). She was a quiet, unobtrusive rebel. Before the end of 1881, however, Martha Luther accepted a proposal of marriage, prompting Charlotte Perkins to close her diary by describing the year as one "in which I knew the sweetness of a perfect friendship and have lost it forever. . . . This year I attained my majority—may I never lose it" (L, 81).

Within a month, she began to compromise her independence. On 12 January of the new year, Charlotte Perkins met Charles Walter Stetson, an aspiring artist. Seventeen days later, he proposed marriage. At first, she declined the offer, though she admitted to Stetson that "You are the first man I have met whom I recognize as an equal; and that is saying a good deal for me. I would call you grandly superior, but that I am fighting just now against a heart-touched woman's passion of abnegation."[9] Even forty years later, in her autobiography, she described Walter Stetson as "quite the greatest man, near my own age, that I had ever known" (*L*, 82). But she had resolved not to marry, at least for a time. She did not wish to repeat her parents' mistake. "If I marry I can never reconsider," she wrote Stetson on 20 February 1882. She preferred "to risk the loss of a few years of possible happiness, rather than risk the endurance of a lifetime's possible pain."[10] She added the next day that "I knew of course the time would come when I must choose between two lives, but never did I dream that it would come so soon, and that the struggle would be so terrible."[11] Walter Stetson pressed his suit. Charlotte Perkins pleaded indecision, torn between "a duty to life and a duty to love."[12] "How often one duty contradicts another," she confessed to him.[13] Forty years later, she still recalled that

On the one hand I knew [that to marry] was normal and right in general, and held that a woman should be able to have marriage and motherhood, and do her work in the world also. On the other, I felt strongly that for me it was not right, that the nature of the life before me forbade it, that I ought to forego the more intimate personal happiness for complete devotion to my work. (*L*, 83)

Nevertheless, she finally capitulated to convention, if not to love. Charlotte Perkins and Walter Stetson were married in Providence on 2 May 1884. A few days before the wedding, the bride read John Stuart Mill's *The Subjection of Women*.[14]

Breakdown

Charlotte Perkins Stetson faced a far greater adjustment to marriage than did her husband. She had been socially and economically independent and had aspired to a career; suddenly, because she adopted a traditional role, she was in charge of keeping house and preparing meals. A week after the wedding, she confided to her diary a hint of apprehension: she had suggested that her husband "pay me for my services; and he much dislikes the idea. I am grieved at offending him; mutual misery. Bed and cry."[15] "Something was going wrong from the first," she wrote later (L, 88). Only a few weeks after her marriage, moreover, Charlotte Perkins Stetson learned that she was pregnant. Walter Stetson, neither cruel nor imperious nor inordinately fastidious, was perplexed by the fits of depression that began to grip his wife, though she would later acknowledge she could not have asked for a "lover more tender, a husband more devoted" than he (L, 87–88). The conventions governing marriage, not the personality of her partner, grated on her. The "immutable submission" demanded of "dutiful house-wives," as she explained, "bred rebellion in me" (L, 85).

She framed her predicament in her first published poem, "In Duty Bound," written in late 1883 and printed in the *Woman's Journal* for 12 January 1884—ironically, the anniversary of her introduction to Walter Stetson:

> In duty bound, a life hemmed in
>   Whichever way the spirit turns to look;
> No chance of breaking out, except by sin;
>   Not even room to shirk—
>   Simply to live, and work.
>
> An obligation pre-imposed, unsought,
>   Yet binding with the force of natural law;
> The pressure of antagonistic thought;
>   Aching within, each hour,
>   A sense of wasting power.
>
> A house with roof so darkly low
>   The heavy rafters shut the sunlight out;
> One cannot stand erect without a blow;
>   Until the soul inside
>   Cries for a grave—more wide.
>
> A consciousness that if this thing endure,
>   The common joys of life will dull the pain;
> The high ideals of the grand and pure
>   Die, as of course they must,
>   Of long disuse and rust.
>
> That is the worst. It takes supernal strength
>   To hold the attitude that brings the pain;

> And they are few indeed but stoop at length
> To something less than best,
> To find, in stooping, rest.
>
> (*ITOW*, 33–34)

This early lyric seems an especially transparent gloss on Charlotte Perkins Stetson's own plight toward the end of 1883. The marital institution ("this thing") is depicted as a penal institution, the home a prison, and the stifled mate an inmate. Images of restraint and confinement are expressed in a lockstep meter. The prisoner must observe a conjugal and reproductive "obligation" which has been "pre-imposed" by the canons of "natural law." Meanwhile, she senses other alternatives or "high ideals" to which she might devote her life and regrets her "wasting power," realizing full well that "few indeed" escape compromise or acquiescence. Even at twenty-three, Charlotte Perkins Stetson successfully translated her misgivings about marriage and the home into verse.

The Stetsons' domestic problems were compounded with the birth, on 23 March 1885, of their daughter, Katharine Beecher. To the duties of wife were added those of mother, and Charlotte Perkins Stetson broke under the accumulated weight. "Every morning the same hopeless waking," she wrote in her diary, "the same weary drag. To die mere cowardice. Retreat impossible, escape impossible."[16] Her dark thoughts turned to self-accusation and self-mortification. "You did it yourself! You had health and strength and hope and glorious work before you—and you threw it all away," she angrily reproached her objectified, "normal" self. "You were called to serve humanity, and you cannot serve yourself. No good as a wife, no good as a mother, no good at anything. And you did it yourself!" Meanwhile, she nursed the baby and, for five months, "instead of love and happiness," she felt "only pain. . . . Nothing was more utterly bitter than this, that even motherhood brought no joy" (*L*, 91–92).

The marriage was like a rope pulled taut. By August 1885, to forestall more misery, Walter Stetson offered "to let me go free," as his wife wrote in her diary, "but he cannot see how irrevocably bound I am, for life, for life. No, unless he die and the baby die, or he change or I change, there is no way out."[17] At last they agreed to a trial separation to relax the strain of the marriage and, in October, Charlotte Perkins Stetson railed west to Utah to see her brother Thomas, to San Francisco to visit her father, and on to Pasadena to

stay with her old friend Grace Ellery Channing. During her holiday
from domestic chores, she rallied both physically and emotionally.
She collaborated with Grace Channing on the writing and production
of amateur theatricals, and she reveled in the work, however trivial.
As she wrote Martha Luther Lane from Pasadena on 4 January 1886,
"In despair of ever getting well at home I suddenly undertook this
journey. It has already done me an immense amount of good, and I
expect to return in the spring as well as I ever shall be."[18] "I re-
covered so fast," she later wrote, "that I was taken for a vigorous
young girl. Hope came back, love came back, I was eager to get
home to husband and child, life was bright again" (L, 94). She re-
turned east in March.

Unfortunately, within a month of her arrival, she had slipped once
more into the Slough of Despond. "This was a worse horror than before," she wrote later, "for now I saw the stark fact—that I was well
while away and sick while at home" (L, 95). One of the problems, as
she noted obliquely in *Women and Economics,* was the familiarity of
domestic routine that bred contempt: "Even the friendship which
may have existed between husband and wife before marriage is often
destroyed by that relation and its economic complications. They have
not time to talk about things as they used: they are too near together" (W&E, 310). Despite her illness, Stetson found time to write
a poem, "The Answer," which dramatized in Darwinian terms her
own struggle for survival and the fate she feared was hers. Like most
of her early verse, the poem develops by analogy. In the first stanza,
a man builds a house in a meadow and contracts a fatal fever there.
In the second, a reformer spends a life in a vain attempt to ameliorate
conditions. Both hear in their death throes the mocking refrain of
Nature: "I teach by killing; let the others learn." Similarly the final
stanza:

> A maid was asked in marriage. Wise as fair,
> She gave her answer with deep thought and prayer,
> Expecting, in the holy name of wife,
> Great work, great pain, and greater joy, in life.
> She found such work as brainless slaves might do,
> By day and night, long labor, never through;
> Such pain—no language can her pain reveal;
> It had no limit but her power to feel;
> Such joy—life left in her sad soul's employ
> Neither the hope nor memory of joy.

Helpless, she died, with one despairing cry,—
"I thought it good; how could I tell the lie?"
And answered Nature, merciful and stern,
"I teach by killing; let the others learn."
(*ITOW*, 2 4)

The lyric was widely copied and the poet subsequently awarded a year's subscription to the *Woman's Journal*.

Charlotte Perkins Stetson struggled valiantly to maintain a separate identity in addition to those of wife and mother. She attended her first suffrage convention in the fall of 1886, publicly embraced dress-reform in an article for the *Woman's Journal* in October, and in March 1887 began to write an occasional column for the *Providence People*, a weekly labor paper. In early winter, moreover, she began "a course of reading on women" that included Margaret Fuller's *Women in the Nineteenth Century*.[19] Nevertheless, her health continued to deteriorate as long as she lived and worked in the home. Finally, in the spring of 1887, she went to Philadelphia to take the "rest cure" prescribed by S. Weir Mitchell, a prominent physician and part-time novelist, "the greatest nerve specialist in the country" at the time. "I was put to bed and kept there," she later recalled. Mitchell's therapy was, in essence, designed to reduce a female patient to the state of childlike docility. As Ann Douglass has explained, Mitchell's method was almost universally applauded because most American physicians at the time "tended unconsciously to see the neuralgic ailments of their female patients as a threatening and culpable shirking of their duties as wives and mothers, and to look upon those duties as the cure, not the cause, of the illness."[20] For over a month, Stetson was petted, treated to large meals and daily massages by a nurse, and then she was sent home by Mitchell with this solemn advice: "Live as domestic a life as possible. Have your child with you all the time. Lie down an hour after each meal. Have but two hours' intellectual life a day. And never touch pen, brush, or pencil as long as you live" (*L*, 95–96). Her illness, according to Mitchell's standard diagnosis, was rooted in her failure to be feminine—that is, to be passive and self-sacrificial. His prescription echoed Mary Perkins's demand thirteen years earlier that her daughter leash her imagination. To be "cured," to regain her mental equilibrium, she was asked to renounce ambition, to submit to her family, to acquiesce to the "blessings" which accrued to her as wife and mother.

She observed the regimen religiously throughout the summer of 1887 "and came so near the border line of utter mental ruin that I could see over" (*CPGR,* 20). Ambition warred with middle-class convention. "The mental agony grew so unbearable," she later reflected in her autobiography, "that I would sit blankly moving my head from side to side—to get out from under the pain." At the nadir of her illness, "I made a rag baby, hung it on a doorknob and played with it. I would crawl into remote closets and under beds—to hide from the grinding pressure of that profound distress." At last, in the fall of 1887, "in a moment of clear vision," Charlotte and Walter Stetson agreed to separate as soon as possible and to divorce when circumstances would permit. Like the troubled marriage of Mary and Frederick Perkins, their union was complicated by the possibility of more children. "There was no quarrel, no blame for either one, never an unkind word between us," she concluded, "but it seemed plain that if I went crazy it would do my husband no good, and be a deadly injury to my child" (*L,* 96). In "To the Young Wife," a poem written in self-admonishment about this time, she more fully expressed her dissatisfaction with domestic drudgery and justly itched for independence:

> Are you content, you pretty three-years' wife?
> Are you content, and satisfied to live
> On what your loving husband loves to give,
> And give to him your life?
>
> Are you content with work,—to toil alone,
> To clean things dirty and to soil things clean;
> To be a kitchen-maid, be called a queen,—
> Queen of a cook-stove throne?
> . . . .
>
> Have you forgotten how you used to long
> In days of ardent girlhood, to be great,
> To help the groaning world, to serve the state,
> To be so wise—so strong?
>
> And are you quite convinced this is the way,
> The only way a woman's duty lies—
> Knowing all women so have shut their eyes?
> Seeing the world to-day?
> . . . .

What holds you? Ah, my dear, it is your throne,
Your paltry queenship in that narrow place,
Your antique labors, your restricted space,
Your working all alone!

Be not deceived! 'T is not your wifely bond
That holds you, nor the mother's royal power,
But selfish, slavish service hour by hour—
A life with no beyond!
(*ITOW*, 129–31)

The break did not occur at once. Charlotte Perkins Stetson vacationed for several months, collaborated on another play with her visiting friend Grace Channing, and disposed of family property to finance her move. Finally, on 8 October 1887, a year after reaching her decision, she boarded a train for Pasadena with her daughter, her mother, and Grace Channing in tow. Her husband would follow two months later and remain in Pasadena for a year, but the attempt at reconciliation would come to naught. She had discharged her duty to love. She might now begin to live.

Literary Apprenticeship

Stetson's professional career began with her arrival in California. She had written poetry for years, but few of her poems had reached print, only "two or three bits" before marriage, "a half-dozen or so" over the next six years. She had resolved to earn her living in part as a writer, however, and in her "first year of freedom" she published, by her own estimate, "some thirty-three short articles, and twenty-three poems, besides ten more child verses" (*L,* 111). She supplemented her income by teaching a class of "some ten or twelve ladies, at five dollars a head, ten lessons" in "modern literature, its causes and effects."[21] She approached the study of literature, like Newton the fallen apple, as a problem in physics.

Her literary theory was, fundamentally, an unapologetic defense of didacticism. The author should instruct the reader, she averred in one of the first essays she published upon moving west, and as readers "we should consider our intentions, the use to which we mean to put our reading." She loosed especial wrath upon the genre of sentimental romance, for the "love story, however much reason and experience may deny," invariably exaggerates the romantic expectations of its impressionable readers, mostly young women.[22] She wasted little patience on works whose authors tinker with point of view or turn well many a felicitous phrase. "I don't care much for [Robert Louis] Stevenson as a whole," she admitted, for example. "I admire, praise, respect, but don't like him. Technique of any sort is a poor thing to me without something behind it. 'Dr. Jekyll' now has my heartiest approval and enjoyment; but much of Stevenson's works seems to me to be done just because he *can!*" Similarly, she expressed misgivings about W. D. Howells's realistic novels of manners: "His work is exquisite, painfully exquisite, but save for that Chinese delicacy of workmanship it seems to me of small artistic value. And its truth is that of the elaborate medical chart, the scientific photograph. . . . I never heard him credited with what seems to be his real purpose—a biting moralism."[23] She scorned dilettantism and the principle of "art for art's sake." Indeed, her friend Charles Lummis, the editor of *Land of Sunshine,* later described her own literary style as "white-hot metal in a sand mold, and no filing."[24] She was interested, above all, in the effect or cash-value of a work.

On the other hand, Stetson approved without qualification literary works which doubled as reform tracts, such as the allegorical fiction of the South African feminist Olive Schreiner. "Olive Schreiner is not merely a writer, or even merely a great writer," she once observed. "She is something far more important—a great thinker. Such minds as hers, appearing from age to age, clarify and rearrange the world's thoughts. She is essentially a poet, both in the sense that the poet is a seer, and in the musical majesty of her forms of expression."[25] Stetson recommended to friends Schreiner's first and best-known novel, *The Story of an African Farm* (1883), whose protagonist has been called "the first wholly feminist" heroine in the English novel.[26] She especially admired Schreiner's collection *Dreams* (1890), in particular "The Sunlight Lay Across My Bed," an anticapitalist parable, and "Three Dreams in a Desert," a "marvellous picture of woman's life in past, present and future" that she occasionally quoted to friends.[27] She eventually declared, with pardonable hyperbole, that *Dreams* "will live for centuries" among the classics of literature, for Schreiner displayed "in this work greater mastery of the allegorical than any writer since the Hebrews" and exercised an "art which gives world visions in single sentences." Stetson also thought a later novel, *Trooper Peter Halket of Mashonaland* (1897), "proved dangerously effective in its condemnation" of the Boer War it shortly anticipated.[28] In all, such fiction as Schreiner's was an effective weapon on several fronts in the campaign for reform.

Her own early stories were designed to be no less didactic. Most were written for such progessive but ill-paying papers as the socialist *Pacific Monthly* and the *Pacific Rural Press,* the organ of the Grange on the Western Slope. In "A Walk for Two," for example, Stetson approved the conduct of a twenty-one-year-old "tomboy" named Ella Graves who "had a knowledge of the world from wide and varied reading," declares she "would rather teach than marry the best man in town," and then proves the point by leading a feckless suitor on a crisp walk to the crest of a hill overlooking the "little, hard-baked New England town" where she lives. There the rascal tries to impose upon her, "but the arm that was used to racket and rein threw off his hand so that he almost fell."[29] In "The Giant Wistaria," written in March 1890, Stetson lamented the plight of an unmarried Puritan mother, like Hawthorne's Hester Prynne, whose tyrannical parents insist she wed a cousin to legitimize her child. The gothic tale concludes as, years later, a boarder in the house describes the ghost of the young mother as she reenacts her escape.[30] In "The Unexpected," written in April 1890, an ambitious artist named Edouard Charpentier, a Walter Stetson persona, continually begs a beautiful but "prudish New England girl," Mary Greenleaf, to marry him until at length she agrees. The first week of their marriage, he later reflects, "was heaven—and the second was hell!" He soon suspects that his seemingly innocent wife enjoys surreptitious affairs with bohemian artists. He plots to murder her latest lover, only to discover in the melodramatic climax that she is also an artist, indeed a better one than he. Her presumed "lover" is but her model, the bohemian den where they meet her studio.[31] In "My Poor Aunt," written in July 1890, the protagonist Kate Bennett aspires at the age of twenty-one to a literary life, but her mother and an aunt conspire to marry her to the first eligible suitor who happens along. On her part, poor Kate did not wish to wed but weighed no alternative. "I did not know what I could look forward to but this or some other marriage," she complains. She feels compelled for reasons of duty and economy to marry a man repulsive to her until, at an opportune moment, another aunt, "the picture of health, happiness, and success," the owner and editor of a small Western newspaper, arrives to offer her a job and her freedom.[32] In each story, Stetson sympathetically portrayed a rebellious young woman who resists the demand that she marry. Each

is the fable of an independent woman. Each also silhouettes the author's frame of mind during her "first year of freedom." Ella Graves,
Mary Greenleaf, and Kate Bennett are idealized versions of Charlotte
Perkins, their stories mental scenarios whereby the author at age
thirty corrected her own mistake at twenty-one, in the first case by
refusing to marry, in the second by pursuing a career of her own, and
in the third by both refusing to marry *and* pursuing a career. Like the
unwed Puritan mother, moreover, Stetson in 1890 risked a soiled
reputation and social ostracism as a single parent. Her fiction was au-
tobiographically moored, though it was by no means literal
autobiography.

Stetson played variations on the feminist theme in other apprenticeship pieces. In such dialogues as "A Dramatic View," "Dame Nature Interviewed," and "Society and the Philosopher," all published
in *Kate Field's Washington* in 1890, she transcribed fanciful debates on
the so-called "woman question" between conservative and progressive
types. Moreover, with her personal liberation she chose to emphasize
in her verse the potential rather than the plight of oppressed womanhood, as in a popular lyric written in 1889:

> She walketh veiled and sleeping,
> For she knoweth not her power;
> She obeyeth but the pleading
> Of her heart, and the high leading
> Of her soul, unto this hour.
> Slow advancing, halting, creeping,
> Comes the Woman to the hour!—
> She walketh veiled and sleeping,
> For she knoweth not her power.
>   (*ITOW*, 125)

Similarly, in "Women of To-day," published in the *Woman's Journal*
in the spring of 1890, she adjured her readers, "Mothers and Wives
and Housekeepers," to "dare to know / The thing you are!" and to
welcome the "women of the future" (*ITOW*, 128–29). Stetson also
collaborated with Grace Channing on another pair of drawing-room
comedies, "A Pretty Idiot" and "Changing Hands," about the modern battle of the sexes. The dialogue was biting, if not witty. In the
first play, the title character defines her femme ideal as "strong, free,
self-reliant, independent—with both intellect and muscle" and "a career of her own." A snob retorts, "Heaven forbid! You are describing

a man!"[33] Despite its faults of construction, both the New York impresario Charles Frohman and the actress Annie Russell later expressed interest in the play.[34]

The sale would have been a windfall. Stetson eked so precarious a livelihood from teaching and writing during her years in Pasadena that, even in the balmy climate of southern California, she was slow to recover her health. In August 1889, in the midst of the attempted reconciliation with Walter Stetson, she complained to a friend that "the weakness of brain which has so devastated my life for the past five years still holds very largely, and while I can do considerable work of a kind which dominates me at the time, or which necessity demands, yet ordinary labor or obligation goes neglected."[35] At least in her own opinion, she would never entirely regain her strength. As a result of her breakdown in the late 1880s and the stress of her work in the early 1890s, she believed she suffered "a lasting loss of power, . . . a laboriously acquired laziness foreign to both temperament and conviction, a crippled life" (*L,* 98). Fortunately, there was a saving grace. She ever after acknowledged that her friend and collaborator "Grace Channing saved what there is of me. Grace Channing pulled me out of living death, set me on my staggering feet, helped me to get to work again, did more than I can say to make me live." Moreover, she had "learned a great deal" during the "long dreary years of illness and melancholy."[36] In the fall of 1890, self-reliant once more, she struggled with the task of re-creating the horrors of her illness in a work of fiction. The result would be a tour de force of psychological realism.

"The Yellow Wall-paper"

Like Stetson's other fiction, "The Yellow Wall-paper" was avowedly didactic, a work of "pure propaganda" as she once described it to W. D. Howells.[37] The narrator, as the reader soon discovers, suffers from severe postpartum depression. With her husband John, a "physician of high standing" who has diagnosed her malady as a "slight hysterical tendency," she has moved for the summer to a rented seaside estate where she might enjoy complete rest. She has been relieved of all domestic duties, including child care and housekeeping, and "absolutely forbidden to 'work' until I am well again" (*CPGR,* 4). Much as Mary Perkins and Weir Mitchell had earlier counseled the author to abandon her imaginary world and to renounce her artistic ambitions, the narrator's husband cautions her "not to give way to fancy in the least. He says that with my imaginative power and habit of story-making, a nervous weakness like mine is sure to lead to all manner of excited fancies" (*CPGR*, 7). In case of protracted recovery, he has promised to "send me to Weir Mitchell in the fall" for further treatment of the same kind. But the narrator objects to this therapy, however well-intentioned, and quietly rebels against the authority which sanctions it. She believes "that congenial work, with excitement and change, would do me good." Indeed, "I think sometimes that if I were only well enough to write a little it would relieve the press of ideas and rest me" (*CPGR*, 7). Like Mitchell, however, John "hates to have me write a word" and "started the habit of making me lie down for an hour after each meal." Despite the prohibition on mental labor, she records her impressions in a diary.

At John's insistence, the narrator settles into an old nursery in the garret of the mansion, a room replete with barred windows opening onto the gardens below, an immobile bedstead, and patterned yellow paper peeling from the walls. At first the wallpaper repels her: "It is dull enough to confuse the eye in following, pronounced enough constantly to irritate and provoke study, and when you follow the lame uncertain curves for a little distance they suddenly commit suicide— plunge off at outrageous angles, destroy themselves in unheard-of contradictions" (*CPGR*, 5). As Sandra Gilbert and Susan Gubar suggest, the "paper surrounds the narrator like an inexplicable text, censorious and overwhelming as her physician husband."[38] In the course of several torpid weeks, however, she begins to discern a "subpattern in a different shade" hidden in the paper. "There are things in that paper that nobody knows but me," she writes. In places she sees "a strange, provoking, formless sort of figure that seems to skulk about behind that silly and conspicuous front design" (*CPGR*, 8). She lies on the immovable bed by the hour and contemplates the pattern. "I start," as she explains, "at the bottom, down in the corner over there where it has not been touched, and I determine for the thousandth time that I *will* follow that pointless pattern to some sort of a conclusion" (*CPGR*, 9). Every few days, she writes of her discoveries in the diary she otherwise conceals in her room. Thus the reader may trace the trajectory of her descent into madness.

The narrator gradually detects the distinct pattern of a crouching woman whose image is infinitely multiplied in the dim shapes. In the moonlight, when the shadows of the bars on the windows fall across the walls, the woman seems to be imprisoned and "in the very shady spots she just takes hold of the bars and shakes them hard." But in daytime the woman seems to escape. "I have watched her sometimes away off in the open country, creeping as fast as a cloud shadow in a wind" (*CPGR*, 16). Eventually the narrator begins to project her own identity onto the figure. One night, she/they peel yards of paper from the walls of the garret prison. As the story ends, the physician-husband breaks into the room to discover the narrator, whose identification with her *Doppelgänger* is complete, creeping about the floor on all fours. She even refers to her "other" self, John's wife, in third person: " 'I've got out at last,' " she declares, " 'in spite of you and Jane. And I've pulled off most of the paper, so you can't put me back!' " In an ironic reversal of the clichéd feminine swoon, the man faints to the floor "so that I had to creep over him every time!" (*CPGR*, 19).

Obviously, like her other early fiction, "The Yellow Wall-paper" was loosely based on Stetson's own experience. To her credit, however, she crafted the tale with care. "When my awful story 'The Yellow Wallpaper' comes out," she proudly wrote Martha Luther Lane, "you must try & read it. Walter says he has read it *four* times, and thinks it the most ghastly tale he ever read. Says it beats Poe," whose tales she had recently reread.[39] According to her manuscript log, on 17 June 1890 she mailed a copy of the story to the editors of *Scribner's,* who quickly declined it. On 28 August she mailed the manuscript to W. D. Howells, who had recently written to express his admiration of her work. Howells forwarded it to Horace Scudder, his successor as editor of the *Atlantic Monthly* who, to Howells's dismay, rejected it with a curt note (*L,* 119). Through the agency of Henry Austin, to whom she sent the manuscript in October 1890, Stetson eventually placed the story with the *New England Magazine,* where it appeared in the January 1892 issue.

The story sparked immediate controversy. Although a reviewer for the *Boston Transcript* dismissed it in one sentence as "very paragraphic and very queer generally,"[40] many early readers considered it a tale of the grotesque, "The Fall of the House of Usher" told from the point of view of the Lady Madeline. Howells shivered over it in manuscript,[41] while Anne Montgomerie wrote in the *Conservator* that the "simple, serious, sly, fascinating, torturing" story "grows and increases with a perfect crescendo of horror," and a reviewer for *Literature* deemed it "worthy of a place beside some of the weird masterpieces of Hawthorne and Poe."[42] A physician wrote the *Transcript* to complain that it "hold[s] the reader in morbid fascination to the end" and to ask whether "such literature should be permitted in print," at least "without protest, without severest censure."[43] On the other hand, another physician wrote the author to commend her "detailed account of incipient insanity." Stetson sent a copy of the story to Weir Mitchell, who deigned not to reply, although years later he reportedly told a friend, "I have altered my treatment of neurasthenia since reading 'The Yellow Wallpaper.' "[44] "If that is a fact," Charlotte Perkins Gilman added in her autobiography, "I have not lived in vain" (*L,* 121).

Certainly the story attracted a cult of readers. It was reprinted in 1899 by Small, Maynard & Co. of Boston as a chapbook bound in sulphurous-yellow board covers resembling the wallpaper. Howells wrote the author a few months before his death in 1920 to request permission to "use your terrible story of 'The Yellow Wall Paper' in a book which I am making for Messrs. Boni and Liveright. . . . You will be in the best company I know, and I hope you will not curdle their blood past liquefying. I wish to pay due recognition to the supreme awfulness of your story in my introduction."[45] Gilman was "pleased and honored" to grant permission,[46] and Howells was as good as his word, including the tale in his collection of *Great Modern American Stories* (1920). H. P. Lovecraft subsequently pronounced it one of the great "spectral tales" in American literature (*CPGR,* xvii). The story was again reprinted in *Golden Book* in 1933 and in a Finnish translation in 1934. With the revival of interest in Gilman's works over the past decade, it has been increasingly anthologized.

Unfortunately, the autobiographical sources of the story have led some modern readers to conclude that "The Yellow Wall-paper" is unvarnished memoir. "The story was wrenched out of Gilman's own life," Elaine Hedges avers, for example.[47] "I am taking the liberty of using 'The Yellow Wall-paper' quite literally as autobiographical material," Mary A. Hill similarly acknowledges.[48] Ironically, the author earlier warned readers to beware the temptation to commit this autobiographical fallacy. Though the narrator suffers from an illness "beginning something as mine did" and which is "treated as Dr. S. Weir Mitchell treated me," Stetson imagined in the story the "inevitable result" of the regimen she had abandoned after three months (*L,* 119). In "A Walk for Two" she had envisioned an alternative past in the person of a protagonist who refused to marry at twenty-one. In "The Yellow Wall-paper" she conceived an alternative future through the eyes of a narrator who continued the rest cure until she was consumed by insanity. As she explained, "I wrote *The Yellow Wallpaper*, with its embellishments and additions, to carry out the ideal." She explicitly noted discrepancies between her own experience and that of "Jane": "I never had hallucinations or objections to my mural decorations" (*CPGR*, 20).

Incredibly, the story "anticipated its own reception," as Annette Kolodny has suggested.[49] Much as the narrator strains to decipher the hieroglyphics she discerns in the paper, early readers of the tale discovered only the conventions of horror and some later readers recognized only the elements of autobiography in it. Even Stetson professed to have written "The Yellow Wall-paper" simply to protest Mitchell's rest cure. None of these interpretations, however, fully comprehends the story. No reader, at least, "made the connection between the insanity and the sex, or sexual role, of the victim" and "no one explored the story's implication for male-female relationships in the nineteenth century."[50] Only feminist readings recently advanced by Kolodny and others, it would seem, adequately decode the fiction.

The narrator of "The Yellow Wall-paper," as these readers emphasize, is trapped in a prison which is at once marital-institutional and linguistic. She is "in duty bound" by the authority of her physician-husband to forsake book and pen. John both reads to her and forbids her from writing, whereupon Jane begins to read in the patterned wallpaper dim inferences or "sprawling outlines" of her own predicament and to record in her diary her desperate bid for emancipation. As Kolodny observes, the narrator has been denied freedom to read and write "ostensibly for her own good" and, "in the course of accommodating herself to that deprivation, comes more and more to experience her self as a text." From her fixed bedstead, symbol of her static sexuality, she watches "her own psyche writ large" on the wall. Peeling away the paper is tantamount to crumbling the walls of her linguistic Jericho. Thus the narrator's descent into madness becomes, according to Jean Kennard, "a way to health" or "a rejection of and escape from an insane society." Her triumph "is symbolized by the overcoming of John, who is last seen fainting on the floor as his wife creeps over him."[51] Neither morbid nor grotesque, the story at its close seems to fulfill Stetson's earlier prophecy in the poem "She Walketh Veiled and Sleeping": "Slow advancing, halting, creeping, / Comes the Woman to the hour!"

Significantly, Charlotte Perkins Stetson would not write again a

story as good as "The Yellow Wall-paper," as if she belatedly heeded,
however unconsciously, the earlier demands that she restrain her
flights of fancy. Even as she was writing the story, she wrestled with
the private demons that visited her during the summer of 1887. A
week after completing the final draft, she noted in her diary that she
had accidentally taken an "overdose of acid phosphate," a stimulant,
which unsettled her nerves.[52] Like many another Victorian, she seems
to have equated madness with inspiration. To organize her life, she
soon turned from imaginative re-creations of personal experience to
activism on behalf of social and political ideals.

Nationalism

Throughout her career, Charlotte Perkins Stetson preached the gospel of a new dispensation. She originally formulated her social critique and reform program in the 1890s while serving an apprenticeship
as a propagandist for Nationalism, and she would exude a brand of
millennial optimism the rest of her life. Unfortunately, her early career as a Nationalist poet and lecturer has been virtually ignored. The
California labor leader Eugene Hough observed in 1897 that Stetson
"came into the field of battle by way of what is known as the 'Nationalist movement,' "[53] but such a bland statement has rarely been
elaborated. Mary Wilhelmine Williams noted Stetson's work as a
Nationalist in a single sentence in a biographical sketch in the *Dic-
tionary of American Biography,* for example.[54] In the only major biography published to date, Mary A. Hill endeavors to repair this
neglect, but her analysis is marred by a failure to date and detail fully
Stetson's activities as a Nationalist. As Anne Firor Scott has noted,
"Hill is more at home with [Stetson's] inner life than with the social
history which shaped her career."[55] Thus, in her account, Stetson's
tenure in the movement seems short-lived, her loyalties temporarily
divided among Nationalism and other reforms more explicitly feminist.[56] In fact, Stetson was intensely and almost exclusively active in
the Nationalist movement for nearly three years, and she closed this
period of her career only when Nationalism, like Holmes's one-hoss
shay, ground to a sudden halt and collapsed into irrelevance.

   In the textbook of Nationalism, the utopian romance *Looking Backward* (1888), Edward Bellamy contrasted the class conflict and cut-
throat competition endemic to Gilded Age America with the
socialism of twenty-first-century America which he conceived as a

cooperative commonwealth. As Bellamy's protagonist Julian West discovers upon awakening from a century-long sleep, all industries have been nationalized, all citizens enjoy economic and sexual equality, and the changes have occurred gradually, peacefully, without recourse to armed revolution as Marx had anticipated. In particular, Bellamy predicted that an advanced civilization would guarantee full rights to women, though the women in his story are but sentimentalized helpmeets. As Julian West's advisor Doctor Leete declares, "Women are a very happy race nowadays, as compared with what they ever were before in the world's history, and their power of giving happiness to men has been of course increased in proportion." Still, women in this utopia are economically independent, freed of the burden of household chores. All domestic services, including washing and cooking, have been socialized.[57]

Bellamy's romance, however silly it may seem to modern readers, inspired upon its publication thousands of quixotic socialists who organized a remarkable reform movement under the banner of Nationalism. Within a few weeks of its publication, Nationalist Clubs had sprouted in major cities throughout the country and, in May 1889, a monthly magazine entitled the *Nationalist* was launched in Boston under official auspices. Though it suspended publication in April 1891 for financial reasons—circulation was small and advertising revenues predictably puny—Bellamy had anticipated its failure and launched a successor journal, the weekly *New Nation,* in January 1891. From the beginning, moreover, Nationalism thrived in the fertile soil of California, even more than in its native New England. By the summer of 1889, twenty-three clubs were forming in the state. An organ of the movement, the *California Nationalist,* began to appear in February 1890 and was soon followed by the *Weekly Nationalist.* By May 1890, over a hundred clubs existed nationwide, with forty-seven of them in California. During the next month, sixteen more clubs were founded across the country, over half of them in California. By November, the highwater mark of the movement, 158 clubs were chartered in all, sixty-five of them in California. As Stetson later recalled, "California is a state peculiarly addicted to swift enthusiasms. . . . In 1890 the countryside was deeply stirred by Bellamy's *Looking Backward"* (*L,* 122).

The movement successfully recruited many women to its ranks during these months by promising the abolition of sex-slavery. With the advent of the "new nation," as one feminist member explained,

women in marital partnerships would no longer be economically subservient to men. Thus every woman ought to join the movement because "Nationalism breaks the strongest fetter which binds woman,
viz., her material dependence of man, and makes her his helpmeet as
an equal and independent partner, accomplishing by economic enfranchisement what political enfranchisement alone could but par-
tially do."[58] In April 1891, the California Nationalists ran candidates
for Congress in two of the six districts and polled 1 1/4 percent of
the total votes cast in the state. The movement soon floundered, however, especially in the wake of its support of the People's party in the
1892 elections. It languished as a political force even before the Panic
of 1893 and subsequent depression eroded much of its remaining
membership. In retrospect, Nationalism often seems little more than
a flurry of parlor socialism, an agitation akin to the single-tax movement or, perhaps, a thin chapter in the lives of such prominent sup-
porters as W. D. Howells, Edward Everett Hale, and Daniel De
Leon. But its long-term effects were salutory, if only because it pro-
vided Stetson with her first major public forum.

It would seem that she slipped into the orbit of Nationalism almost accidentally. She had read *Looking Backward* soon after its publication, to judge from her correspondence. "I grant that Bellamy has
no style. I wonder if John the Baptist had," she wrote Martha Luther
Lane. "Is it possible that you see nothing in that book but its poor
execution?"[59] Though intrigued by Bellamy's doctrines, she was not
affiliated with the movement his romance inspired until "one of the
editorial board" of the *Nationalist*,[60] probably her uncle Edward Hale,
solicited a contribution from her. On 1 March 1890, according to her
manuscript log, she submitted a lyric entitled "Similar Cases" to the
magazine which, upon its publication in the April issue, was hailed
as a minor classic of satirical verse.

In the poem, Stetson burlesqued social conservatism in the accents
of a reform Darwinist. First, a prehistoric Eohippus declares his intention to become a horse; next, an ape his intention to become a
man. In both cases, critics ridicule their hopes with the refrain,
"You'd have to change your nature!" In the final stanza, Stetson's
rhetoric rises an octave:

> There was once a Neolithic Man, an enterprising wight,
> Who made his simple implements unusually bright.
> Unusually clever he, unusually brave,
> And he sketched delightful mammoths on the borders of his cave.

To his Neolithic neighbors, who were startled and surprised,
Said he: "My friends, in course of time, we shall be civilized!
We are going to live in cities and build churches and make laws!
We are going to eat three times a day without the natural cause!
We're going to turn life upside-down about a thing called gold!
We're going to want the earth and take as much as we can hold!
We're going to wear a pile of stuff outside our proper skins;
We're going to have Diseases! and Accomplishments!! and Sins!!!"
Then they all rose up in fury against their boastful friend;
For prehistoric patience comes quickly to an end.
Said one: "This is chimerical! Utopian! Absurd!"
Said another: "What a stupid life! Too dull, upon my word!"
Cried all: "Before such things can come, you idiotic child,
You must alter Human Nature"! and they all sat back and smiled.
Thought they: "An answer to that last it will be hard to find."
It was a clinching argument—to the Neolithic Mind!

                                                      (*ITOW*, 95–100)

The poem won Stetson immediate celebrity. Over the next several weeks she would publish two short articles in the *California Nationalist,* another article in the *Weekly Nationalist,* and she would submit three more poems—inexplicably refused—to the *Nationalist* in Boston,[61] but she could count "Similar Cases" the only genuine success among them. Howells, a charter member of the First Nationalist Club of Boston, wrote her on 9 June that "I've read [your poem in the April *Nationalist*] many times with unfailing joy. . . . We have nothing since the Biglow Papers half so good for a good cause as 'Similar Cases.' "[62] Stetson was frankly gratified by his note, and replied to Howells the day she received it that "there is not a man in America whose praise in literature I would rather win!"[63] Thirty years later, she echoed this comment in her autobiography and added that, bolstered by Howells's good opinion, "I felt like a real 'author' at last" (*L,* 122). Edward Hale also congratulated his niece: The poem "is perfect," he wrote her on 15 July 1890. "If I told you all I say of it and all that other people say I should turn your head. The idea was an inspiration." He later told her he thought the poem "a great campaign document."[64] The *New England Magazine,* perhaps at Hale's behest, later reprinted the poem with approbation; Gertrude Franklin Atherton, a Stetson acquaintance, quoted Howells's letter in *Cosmopolitan* and added that "the humor [of the poem] is so sharp and the satire so keen that any member of that sex which claims humor as its special prerogative would be glad to have written it";[65] and the *Nationalist* subsequently reprinted Atherton's comments in praise of the "young author who has rendered such service to the cause of nationalism."[66] Lester Ward, the so-called philosopher of the modern welfare state, pronounced it a "remarkable poem" and the "most telling answer that has ever been made" to conservative Darwinists. When E. L. Godkin publicly attacked Bellamy's utopian scheme, Ward sent a copy of Stetson's poem to him and, later, he even tried his hand at a fourth stanza, in imitation of Stetson.[67] No less a luminary than Ambrose Bierce thought "Similar Cases" a "delightful satire upon those of us who have not the happiness to think that the progress of humanity toward the light is subject to sudden and lasting acceleration."[68] In all, as Stetson concluded her diary for the year 1890, "My whole literary reputation dates . . . mainly from 'Similar Cases.' "[69]

The poem also launched Stetson's career as a public lecturer. One day in the spring of 1890, while riding in a bus in her hometown of Pasadena, she was invited by another passenger to speak before the local Nationalist Club. As she recalled in her autobiography, "This was an entirely new proposition. I had never given a public address nor expected to. But here was an opportunity, not wrong, and I accepted it" (*L,* 122). On 10 June 1890, she completed the manuscript of her lecture, entitled "On Human Nature." On 15 June, she delivered it twice with "Great success" in the storefront meeting room of the Club, and later she repeated it, by invitation, before a private audience. "Edward Bellamy has not invented much. Few people do," she declared. "He has put in popular form the truths of ages, and done it at a time when the whole world was aching for such help." To be sure, the love story in *Looking Backward* is sentimental and contrived, but such complaints are trivial, merely personal jibes: "I have a friend near Boston," Stetson observed, "a highly cultivated woman, who says she does not care for a religion with such a flabby apostle! She does not like [Bellamy's] literary style!"[70] The next issue of the *Weekly Nationalist* praised Stetson's "admirable refutation of the constantly reiterated argument that nothing can be done until we alter human nature."[71] Her reputation as poet and lecturer preceding her, she delivered the same address on 13 July before the First Nationalist Club in Los Angeles to a "tumultuous" reception.[72] Harriet Howe, a feminist writer and member of the program committee at the Los Angeles club, recalled later that "the audience began to interrupt her with frequent applause, their puzzlement at first no doubt being due to hearing valuable ideas from a woman, a woman who had something to say and knew how to say it devoid of all platitudes."[73] The lecture was so popular in Los Angeles that, within two weeks, she rewrote part of it for publication in the *Weekly Nationalist* and for separate distribution as a Nationalist tract.[74]

Soon Stetson was lecturing on alternate Sundays at the Pasadena and Los Angeles clubs on such topics as "Nationalism and the Virtues," "Nationalism and Love," "Nationalism and Religion," and "Nationalism and the Arts," with occasional digressions on dress reform and socialized child care. In her lecture "Why We Want Nationalism," she explicitly defined the goals of the movement: "[Nationalism] is a system of industrial organization by which the whole nation may obtain the greatest wealth with the least exertion," she announced, "and by which the whole nation may equally share in the common necessaries of life." All means of production should be nationalized and administered to provide for the general welfare. She even invoked the authority of her uncle to rationalize the goals of the movement: "As Edward Everett Hale truly says, Nationalism is but the American idea further carried out. Because we want health and freedom and all noble growth and improvement, because we want to see common sense in all departments of human life, because we wan[t] Justice and absolute Rights—that is why we want Nationalism."[75] "It was pleasant work," she would later reflect. "I had plenty to say and the Beecher faculty for saying it" (*L,* 122). She carefully noted in her diary the honoraria she collected for these lectures—usually only three to five dollars per date—but she was undaunted. "I have been told that there has been somewhat of a falling off in interest in Nationalism," she opened a lecture written in December 1890. "To me, who find my interest in Nationalism increasing every day, this seems strange."[76]

In her appeals on behalf of Nationalism, Stetson discussed many rudimentary ideas she elaborated later in her career. In her lecture "The Dress and the Body," for example, she rehearsed the thesis she more fully developed a quarter-century later in *The Dress of Women:* "The clothes of women will not change until the habits of women change."[77] In "Nationalism and the Arts," she outlined her concept of social motherhood: A "Nationalist child," she averred, would be "reared in a child's world, with every best surrounding, best care, best teaching given him by the common sense of the community."[78] Stetson also championed in her Nationalist lectures the economic independence of women, her most characteristic and recurrent theme. With the advent of the New Nation, she explained in 1892, "Women will be independent financially, not of each other, not of the race, but of this revolting condition of dependence upon the man with whom they hold the relation of marriage."[79] She took pains to assure her audience that, though separated from her husband, she preached no doctrine of free love. "Monogamous marriage is our ideal, the perfect and lasting union of two happy human beings," she allowed in "Nationalism and Religion."[80] "I believe in permanent monogamous marriage as the present highest ideal of humanity," she added, with only a hint of equivocation, in another address.[81] The net effect of Nationalism, she concluded, would be to refine the marital institution and raise the standard of virtue, for women in the New Nation would be free to marry for love, not compelled to marry for survival or security. In the New Nation, for the first time in human history, sexual selection would be natural and instinctual, not skewed by base economic motives: "When women are no [longer forced] to maintain themselves by loving [men] in marriage or out—when a man [courts] as a possible lover, but not as 'a good [provider']—when there is not a market on [women] and poverty steadily driving thousands [upon] thousands into that market—then they will be chaste."[82] Soon after joining the Nationalist lecture circuit in the summer of 1890, Stetson even helped to organize a local Pasadena Social Purity Society, a group allied in her view with the larger Nationalist cause.

Especially in 1891 and 1892, at the peak of Stetson's popularity as a Nationalist speaker, local newspapers as well as the Boston *New Nation,* under Bellamy's editorship, publicized her lectures in their pages. One address in Los Angeles was so well-received, for example, that a newspaper there lamented "that its length precludes us from publishing it entire."[83] The *New Nation* praised her work and summarized her lectures on its "Club News" page no less than ten times between 7 February and 6 June 1891, with such encomiums as "very interesting" and "witty and very entertaining" punctuating the reports. The 31 May issue devoted two full paragraphs to her recent address on "Nationalism and the Arts" before the First Nationalist Club in Oakland, an audience which "crowded to its utmost capacity" the local Grand Army hall.[84] The next week, she was described in the pages of the *New Nation* as one "of the ablest speakers in the movement."[85] When Edward Hale toured southern California in February and March of 1891 to lecture on Nationalism, she helped to arrange his itinerary and accompanied him on some his stops, occasionally addressing the audiences in turn. She was, by all accounts, an effective evangelist of the gospel of Nationalism, sincere and single-minded in her commitment to the cause she once declared "the greatest movement of modern times."[86]

In addition to her lecture work throughout the state, Stetson was active in local Nationalist clubs, especially after she moved to Oakland in September 1891 to live with Adeline E. Knapp, a reporter for the *San Francisco Call*. The Oakland club was moribund upon her arrival and, characteristically, she set to work reviving it. Her first convert, in fact, was her friend Knapp. On 18 October, a month after her arrival in the city, she recorded in her diary that she had "a good talk with Delle on Nationalism." On 6 November, she rehearsed a new Nationalism lecture, "What Life Might Be," before the local club and confided to her diary that "Delle is beginning to feel much roused on these questions." A week later, Stetson and Knapp attended a meeting to reorganize the local association, and on 17 November they spent "a happy evening over a constitution for the New Nationalist Club, or, as I have called it the New Nation Club." The next day, at a committee meeting, Knapp was figuratively baptized into the flock. "She is made one of us," Stetson concluded her diary that day. The reorganized club boasted a membership of thirty-six by mid-December, and in early January, at its semiannual business meeting, Stetson was elected the new corresponding secretary and Knapp the librarian.[87] In its next issue, the *New Nation* duly reported that the club had been reorganized and mentioned that Stetson had been elected an officer, adding that she "is at present giving Sunday lectures which are thoroughly nationalistic in their tone."[88] The club soon rented a "nice little hall" at 865 Broadway in Oakland, Stetson noted in her diary, and held its first public meeting there in the evening of 15 January 1892. Stetson delivered a keynote address to the assembly entitled "What is Nationalism?" in which she outlined the immediate purposes of the group: "This club hopes to spread some knowledge of [Nationalism] both by these meetings and the dissemination of literature."[89] The speech was "received with enthusiasm. Very successful indeed."[90] Stetson also served as chair of the program committee, in which office she arranged for such speakers as the iconoclastic poet Edwin Markham, later the author of "The Man with the Hoe," to address the club.[91] Years later, she re-created this period of

her life in a short story, "Mrs. Potter and the Clay Club," in which
the title character became the secretary of a disorganized group of local humanitarians "and did her work with steady accuracy." As Mrs.
Potter "became more widely acquainted, she was put on the membership committee, a position most modestly accepted, but resulting
in a most notable improvement in new members." She also helped
"in the program work, cajoling speakers who did not want to speak,
and repressing some who did; also in carrying out a plan of special
invitations to each lecture, of persons likely to be interested and desirable for membership." Mrs. Potter, as her name suggests, shapes
the organization until "a sense of peace and harmony suffused the res-
urrected club."[92] Unfortunately, Stetson's art did not exactly imitate
life. Her revival of the Oakland club was not crowned with such unqualified success. Over the weeks, in fact, she betrayed irritation with
several club members. She attempted to host a discussion at the hall
on Sunday afternoon, 31 January, for example, but "Too many
cranks" had appeared and she had been forced to "give it up."[93] Significantly, she invoked the same phrase here that she used in her autobiography to describe the repression of her personal fantasy life
when thirteen years old. Eventually, she would forswear the dream of
Nationalism, though she faithfully attended most of the weekly
meetings of the local club in company with Knapp at least through
the spring of 1892.

By early 1891, Stetson had also earned a reputation as a poet of
Nationalism. Edward Hale placed one of her poems, a burlesque of
opposition to the movement entitled "An Anti-Nationalist Wail," in
the *New England Magazine* for December 1890. Another of her early
Nationalist poems, "A Conservative," was printed in *Life,* and several
other pieces, including "Another Conservative," appeared in the *Pacific Monthly,* recently converted to Nationalist principles. When, in
February 1891, she submitted a satirical poem entitled "The Survival
of the Fittest" to the Boston *New Nation,* she received in reply a letter
of acceptance from the editor, Edward Bellamy himself. The poem,
Bellamy informed Stetson, already had been featured in a reading at
the local Nationalist club and, in the wake of "Similar Cases," it had
"quite made your fame hereabouts!" Bellamy added in closing that
"anything you can send me will be most welcome."[94] The poem subsequently appeared in the 14 March 1891, issue of the *New Nation,*
as follows:

In northern zones the ranging bear
Protects himself with fat and hair.
Where snow is deep and ice is stark,
And half the year is cold and dark,
He still survives a clime like that
By growing fur, by growing fat.
These traits, O bear, which thou transmittest
Prove the survival of the fittest!

To polar regions waste and wan
Comes the approaching race of man.
A puny, feeble, little lubber—
He has no fur, he has no blubber.
The scornful bear sat down at ease
To see the stranger starve and freeze;
But lo! the stranger slew the bear,
And ate his fat, and wore his hair!
These deeds, O Man! which thou committest,
Prove the survival of the fittest!

In modern times the millionaire
Protects himself as did the bear.
Where Poverty and Hunger are,
He counts his bullion by the car.
Where thousands suffer, still he thrives,
And after death his Will survives.
The wealth, O Croesus! thou transmittest,
Proves the survival of the fittest!

But lo! some people, odd and funny,
Some men without a cent of money,
The simple, common Human Race,—
Chose to improve their dwelling place!
They had no use for Millionaires;
They calmly said the world was theirs;
They were so wise—so strong—so many—
The Millionaire?—There wasn't any!
These deeds, O Man, which thou committest,
Prove the survival of the fittest!

(*ITOW*, 208–9)

During her period of commitment to the cause of Nationalism, even before she was introduced to the work of Lester Ward, in short, Char-

lotte Perkins Stetson satirized the social-Darwinian apology for laissez-faire capitalism. As Carol Farley Kessler has concluded, Stetson's
light verses "question the basic assumptions that underlie our social
structure and thus have unquestionably radical intent."[95]

As good as his word, Bellamy over a period of three years printed
in the *New Nation* a total of ten poems from Stetson's pen. Indeed, in
the issue dated 24 June 1893, he referred to her as "the poet of nationalism so well known to our readers."[96] Shortly after Stetson sent
him a copy of her verse anthology *In This Our World* in November
1893, Bellamy thanked her for the inscription "which I should be
glad to think it possible to deserve" and added that "I have already
shown my high opinion of your poems on nationalism" by printing
them in the magazine.[97] The earliest verse Stetson submitted to Bellamy, like "The Survival of the Fittest," was light and humorous. In
"The Amoeboid Cell," for example, she dramatized a dialogue between a specialized cell, a component of a larger body which adapts
to changing circumstances and survives, and a primitive amoeboid
cell, an utter individualist who soon dies from exposure. The later
lyrics Stetson contributed to the *New Nation* tend to be more uncon-
ventional, often written in free verse, and solemnly polemical, opening with such declarations as "The nation is the unit" and "Free land
is not enough." Stetson's final poem in the *New Nation* appeared in
the 6 January 1894 issue—less than a month before Bellamy ceased
publication of the magazine. As a regular contributor, moreover,
Stetson predictably lamented its demise: "*The New Nation* is suspended, owing of course, to the pressure of this hardest of hard
years," she remarked. "It is a pity, for never was a reform paper more
clear, simple, logical, well written and well sustained. But it is very
hard to sustain a reform paper whose appreciators are mainly among
the poor."[98] Stetson did not abandon Nationalism, in short. Others
defected, but she remained an active Nationalist until the movement
disintegrated.

For a variety of reasons, to be sure, Stetson curtailed her agitation
on behalf of Nationalism after 1892. Despite official protestations of
sexual equality, most of the clubs observed an unofficial policy of discrimination. "The women in [the Los Angeles] Nationalist Club," as
Harriet Howe reminisced, "were treated with the usual condescension
with which men treat women in all matters supposed to be over
women's heads. The women tired of that treatment."[99] Stetson betrayed similar irritation in a letter to Markham, written in late March

1892, in which she urged the poet "to take a more active interest in the club work. We need so much the effort of wise and capable men, and have so few of them."[100] Also, by the end of 1892 Stetson had begun to quarrel with Adeline Knapp, who would eventually write an antisuffrage tract. "My last love proves even as others," as she closed her diary for the year. "Out of it all I ought surely to learn final detachment from all personal concerns."[101] Moreover, Stetson probably was displeased by public statements of Nationalist leaders asked to comment on reports of her impending divorce. According to the *Boston Globe,* Walter Stetson had accused his estranged wife "of devoting her time to the doctrines of Bellamy" and had disparaged her "crank theories."[102] The story received wide publicity, especially in the Hearst chain of newspapers, in mid-December 1892, though Walter Stetson vociferously denied the statements attributed to him in the *Globe* article. Unfortunately, both L. J. Bridgman, president of the First Nationalist Club in Boston, and Henry R. Legate, president of the Second Nationalist Club, hastened to disavow any association of their economic doctrines with liberal divorce. Bridgman told an interviewer for the *Boston Herald* the day after the story broke that "Neither Bellamy nor Nationalists generally have espoused loosening of marriage ties," and Legate bluntly asserted that "Nationalism has nothing to do with the subject of marriage."[103] So much for the economic independence of women, it would seem. Charlotte Perkins Stetson doubtless read these remarks in the *Boston Herald,* for she saved a clipping of the article among her papers.

Finally, Stetson devoted less time directly to Nationalism in 1893–94 as she filled her agenda with other reform activities. For example, on 5 September 1892, she read a prize essay on the labor movement before the Alameda County Federation of Trades, an organization she subsequently joined. She forwarded a copy of the essay to the *New Nation,* whose editor thoroughly approved its Nationalistic sentiments and excerpted it in the 24 June and 23 September 1893 issues. "As the workers of humanity we hold the world in our hands," she had concluded, "and can make it what we will. Forward, then, in the light of truth and the warmth of mutual love!"[104] Like other Nationalists, Stetson also campaigned for People's party candidates, especially those standing in Oakland municipal elections. She began to contribute Nationalist stories and essays to several local newspapers, such as a feature article on the twentieth-century woman printed in the *San Francisco Call* in May 1893, and by the winter of 1893 she was editing the *Impress,* the magazine of the Pacific Coast Women's Press Asociation.

Stetson continued to advertise Nationalism in that journal. She read *A Traveler from Altruria* and *Letters of an Altrurian Traveler* as they appeared serially in *Cosmopolitan,* admired the Nationalist flavor of Howells's tales of a visitor from an imaginary Christian commonwealth, and took the first opportunities to puff the utopia romances in the pages of the *Impress.* Though she had privately admitted in July 1890 that Howells "never was a favorite of mine," she thought his Altrurian romances wed "the power and grace of high literary art to the force of truth." Such stories as *Looking Backward* and *A Traveler from Altruria,* she added, "have the effect of making every day troubles seem like unbearable terrors."[105] In early January 1895, moreover, she published in the *Impress* a Bellamyesque story, "A Cabinet Meeting," which purported to depict a Cabinet debate in the New Nation on the merits of universal education.[106] In the next issue, she editorially honored Bellamy's "largeness of thought," his "daring imagination, the careful, practical planning of detail, and the imme _uman love" which marked his utopian scheme. "A man who can sway the thought of the age, as Mr. Bellamy has swayed it," she concluded, "is no mean author."[107] In another issue, she announced a forthcoming lecture in San Francisco by the socialist Laurence Gronlund, author of *The Coöperative Commonwealth* (1884), which, she noted, "is believed to have furnished much of the inspiration and the argument on which Bellamy founded his 'Looking Backward' and Howells his 'Traveller from Altruria.' "[108] Stetson and Bellamy subsequently served together as contributing editors to the *American Fabian,* a socialist magazine, for several months beginning in December 1896, and she honored him upon his death in the spring of 1898 by speaking at a memorial service chaired by Howells at the Social Reform Club in New York.[109] In short, Stetson did not part company with Bellamy and his followers in the late 1890s. Their paths often paralleled and sometimes crossed. In *Women and Economics* (1898) and *The Home* (1903), she betrayed the influence of Bellamy and the Nationalist reformers George Duysters and John Pickering Putnam, though she did not mention them by name, by detailing the advantages of kitchenless homes grouped together and "connected by covered ways with [a common] eating-house."[110] In *The Man-Made World* (1910), she echoed Bellamy's prediction that eventually crime will be treated as a "moral disease," not punished retributively: "The world's last prison will be simply a hospital for moral incurables," she wrote (*MMW*, 203).

In later years, long after Nationalism became passé, remembered if at all as an intense but brief enthusiasm, the movement continued to influence the works of Charlotte Perkins Gilman. She continued to refer in print to Bellamy even after she retired from public life at sixty-two. In 1923, in *His Religion and Hers*, she once more explicitly invoked his name: whereas most people are eager to believe in an otherworldly millennium or afterlife, she complained, we tend to ridicule and dismiss this-world utopias submitted for approval in blueprint by Plato, Bellamy, H. G. Wells, and others (*HRH*, 27). And in her autobiography, posthumously published though mostly written in the mid-1920s, she reminisced about the heady days a generation before when, for nearly three years, she shared with other Nationalists a faith in the imminent realization of a utopian dream. Her enthusiasm had waned over the years, but she expressed no regrets. She had served with distinction in the front ranks of the Bellamyite campaign and, more than any other figure active in the movement, she had built a career espousing the Nationalist platform.

Chapter Two
"A Strong-Minded Woman"

Editor of the *Impress*

First the separation from Walter Stetson, next the death of her mother in March 1893, then the separation from Adeline Knapp— even as she attracted public notice Charlotte Perkins Stetson suffered private grief. She cultivated new friends partly to compensate for her losses. In Oakland she lived across Webster Street from Ina Coolbrith, later the poet laureate of California; visited regularly with Eugene Hough, Joaquin Miller, and Edwin Markham; and met Hamlin Garland and James Whitcomb Riley. Harriet Howe remembered her regular evenings "at home" in 1893–94 when she led "a sort of salon" or forum "where various psychological, philosophical, economic, biological and ethical questions were discussed." Stetson "seemed to thrive and expand on these occasions," Howe recalled.[1] Each week she invited such "literati as I can induce to come" to enjoy "some good talking and a bite to eat."[2] One of the recurring themes of the evenings was the accursed monopoly of the Southern Pacific Railroad and the futile crusade to abolish it (*L,* 145–50). Meanwhile, like the penny-a-line newspaperman who narrates her arabesque tale "The Rocking Chair" (1893), she continued to contribute poems, stories, and feature essays—"slow work, unpleasant and ill-paid"[3] —to the *Stockton Mail,* the *San Francisco Call,* the *Oakland Enquirer,* and other local papers. She even began a novelette entitled "A Fallen Sister," since lost.[4]

Daughter Katharine was both burden and ballast. In one of her most popular stories, "The Unnatural Mother," written in June 1893 and thrice reprinted in magazines she later edited,[5] Stetson dramatized her quandary. The title-character, like the author of the story, had "grown up, the somewhat neglected child of a heart-broken" single parent, as "a regular tomboy" (*CPGR,* 58). Her "wild, healthy childhood" made her "very different in her early womanhood from the meek, well-behaved damsels" of the village, and as a result the rumor-mongers "shook their heads and prophesied no good of a girl who was 'queer' " (*CPGR,* 59). To their surprise, she married at last, though "a mighty queer husband she got, too. He was an artist or something" (*CPGR,* 62) She bore "one child, a girl," but according to the gossipy neighbors she "never seemed to have no maternal feelin' at all!" She allowed the child to "roll round in the grass like a puppy" and treated her "worse n' an Injun," though admittedly the child grew into "a great strappin' girl" (*CPGR,* 63). One evening, when the so-called "unnatural mother" saw an earthen dam collapsing, she ran past her own home to warn her neighbors of the imminent disaster—that is, she risked the life of her own child to save the lives of fifteen hundred villagers—and died in the flood after sounding the alarm. A martyr by any other standard, she nevertheless is condemned by the busybodies because, as they assert, "A mother's duty is to her own child!" Only one woman, unmarried and childless at age thirty-six, defends the action: "It does seem to me that she did her duty" (*CPGR,* 65). Like this character, Stetson adjured her readers to stand ready to sacrifice for all humanity.

The story silhouettes her own utilitarian attitude toward motherhood during these years. She felt called to serve the community at large, perhaps at the sacrifice of her own child. She even anticipated the scandal such a decision would provoke. In May 1894, she sent Katharine east to live with Walter Stetson and Grace Channing, who would marry in June. Charlotte Perkins Stetson ever after referred to Channing as her "co-mother," a "second mother" to her daughter "fully as good as the first, better in some ways perhaps." As she later recounted the episode, moreover, she had borne the brunt of sacrifice: "No one suffered from [this arrangement] but myself. This, however, was entirely overlooked in the furious condemnation which followed. I had 'given up my child' " (*L,* 163). Certainly the situation revealed latent contradictions in Stetson's own feminist views. Whereas she preached the equality of the sexes, she also shared the popular assumption that women possess a unique instinct to nurture children. She would write that "Motherhood is not a remote contingency, but the common duty and the common glory of womanhood" (*W&E,* 246) and that "The mother instinct, throughout nature, is one of unmixed devotion, of love and service, care and defense, with no self-interest" (*MMW,* 131). On the one hand, she disparaged the domestic duties, including child care, which fell primarily to women, yoked them to the home, and thus enforced their social inferiority.

Like Ibsen's Nora Helmer, whose example she later cited,[6] Stetson abdicated her cook-stove throne and fled the doll house. Her decision to relinquish custody of Katharine may seem a bold bid to escape, at last and forever, the drudgery of kitchen and laundry. As late as 1975, the nonagenarian Katharine Stetson Chamberlin still claimed that her mother in 1894 had "seized the opportunity to get her freedom by shipping me East."[7] On the other hand, Stetson presumed, correctly, that Grace Channing, not Katharine's father, would bear primary responsibility for rearing the child. As in a zero-sum game, her own freedom was purchased at another's expense.

Like the "unnatural mother" in her story, she rationalized her decision in ruthlessly utilitarian terms. In "The Duty Farthest," written soon after Katharine's departure, she filed a dissent to the majority opinion that a woman is first and always "in duty bound" to her immediate family:[8]

> Finding myself unfit to serve my own,
> I left them, sadly, and went forth alone
>   Unto the world where all things wait to do—
>   The harvest ripe—the laborers but few.
> I studied long to find the wisest way,
> Proved every step, worked on day after day
>   In those great common tasks that need us all
>   But where one's own part is so brief and small
> That no one counts the labor one has spent
> Yet I could see good grow and was content.
>   Ah me! I sighed, for home served lovingly.
>   And lo! the whole round world was home to me.

Occasionally, her resolution slipped: "I tried to reassure myself last night in the dark," she confided to her cousin George Houghton Gilman in 1900, "that after all my real personal duty, biggest of all, was to speak and write. Not at the expense of my child—but it has not been."[9] She was also comforted on such occasions by the examples of her aunt Harriet Beecher Stowe who, she believed, had proved her "value to the world" through "a great book" rather than through the nurture of her children.[10]

She moved to San Francisco, to "a place unsuitable for a child," to pursue "new work" in the spring of 1894 (L, 162). At the time she was serving a term as president of the hundred-strong Pacific Coast Women's Press Association and, for several months past, she had ed-

ited its organ the *Impress*. In May 1894, the same month she sent
Katharine east, she revealed an ambitious plan to assume ownership
of the paper; expand the eight-page monthly to a sixteen-page
weekly; and share editorial duties with Helen Campbell, a fellow Nationalist and a founding member of the National Household Economics Association. Stetson had long hoped to edit a reputable literary
magazine. Years before, shortly after her arrival in Pasadena, she had
printed a prospectus for an illustrated monthly to be called the *Cali-
fornian* and had solicited contributions from her father, her uncle Edward Hale, Charles Dudley Warner, "and other literary lights I
knew," until the sponsor at the last moment "wisely shrank from the
financial risk" and withdrew support for the project (*L,* 124). Now,
by enlarging an established paper, she hoped to make the *Impress* "a
good family weekly," one "not exclusively feminist in tone, but varied and interesting," a paper which would advocate "all truly progressive measures" (*L,* 171, 173).

For twenty weeks, she succeeded admirably. Campbell edited a
home-economics page entitled "The Art of Living" while Stetson
managed the business and contributed "articles, verses, editorials"
and a column on "Every-Day Ethical Problems." She also produced
a seventeen-part series of "Studies in Style" so that her readers might
"develop a wide knowledge and more delicate appreciation of distinctive literary methods," each week printing short fiction or drama in
avowed imitation of such authors as Irving, Poe, Hawthorne, Dickens, Kipling, Maeterlinck, Olive Schreiner, Edward Everett Hale,
George Eliot, Louisa May Alcott, Mary E. Wilkins, Hamlin Garland, Henry James, and Mark Twain. She had read all of them,
through the years, with varying degrees of pleasure. For example, she
was "much displeased" by James's unsympathetic portrayal of feminism in *The Bostonians,* but she found "permanent satisfaction" in
Dickens's social satires *Our Mutual Friend, Hard Times, A Tale of Two
Cities,* and *Little Dorrit.*[11] Some of her imitations were skillfully executed. Years later, for example, her publishers Small and Maynard
reprinted her mock-Maeterlinck in one of their magazines (*L,* 241).

The journal was lively and well-received, at least by the critics
whose testimonials the editors solicited and published. The president
of Stanford University, David Starr Jordan, whom Stetson met in
March 1894, wrote that he found "the paper bright, fresh and clear;
it contains much matter of value, especially to the women of the
coast." Stetson's cousin, Edward Hale, Jr., a professor of English lit-

erature at the University of Iowa, pronounced it "brilliantly written, and full of good things." Local reviewers praised its "admirable literary tone," its "intellectual" appeal, the "distinctive novelty" of the studies in style, even the "bright and radical personality" of its much-maligned editor. The *San Francisco Star,* a single-tax paper, concluded that Stetson's connection with the *Impress* "should be sufficient to ensure its favorable reception."[12]

Unfortunately, the weekly suspended publication after barely four months. Stetson peddled advertisements and enlisted subscription agents to hawk the paper in other cities, but to no avail. Despite its merits, the magazine was no longer underwritten by the P.C.W.P.A., could no longer claim that constituency as an asset, and could not surmount the liability of Stetson's local reputation as a divorced woman and "unnatural mother." "The *Impress* failed, notwithstanding its real excellence, because of unthinking prejudice," Harriet Howe later concluded. "Mrs. Stetson was greatly misunderstood, misjudged, and mistreated in San Francisco."[13] As Stetson herself reflected, "This fiasco was what showed me my standing in that city" (*L,* 173). With the issue of 16 February 1895, the *Impress* ceased publication, a casualty of its editor's notoriety. Stetson was doubtless disappointed, but she was not silenced. She merely broadened her audience. After all, the world, not the bay, was her oyster. She soon became a regular contributor to *Land of Sunshine* but, once burned, she would not again try her hand at editing a magazine until she launched the *Forerunner* in 1909.

In This Our World

Floyd Dell called her "first of all, a poet, an idealist," the author of "the best satirical verses of modern times," but no one seems to have noticed.[14] Even in 1913, when Dell expressed this opinion, her early reputation as a poet had been eclipsed by the long shadows of her later essays. However, Charlotte Perkins Stetson's first book was a collection of vagrant verse, mostly lyrics she had published since 1890, which was applauded in literary circles on both sides of the Atlantic. The first edition of *In This Our World,* printed by two of Stetson's socialist friends and deposited for copyright on 24 October 1893, contained but seventy-three poems and a hundred and twenty pages bound in paper covers reminiscent of Schreiner's *Dreams.* The *vers de société* was divided into three sections: "The World," mostly nature-poems, carols, and prayers; "Woman," feminist hymns, many reprinted from the *Woman's Journal;* and "Our Human Kind," political anthems, most on Nationalist and labor themes.

She sold the anthology for twenty-five cents per copy on consignment in bookstores and by subscription to friends, and it "brought small returns in cash but much in reputation. It was warmly reviewed in certain discerning papers." Frederic Saunders in the *Unity* of Chicago wrote "a particularly appreciative notice" which commended the volume to Unitarian ministers (*I.,* 169). The *San Francisco Star* praised the "intense feeling," "condensed expression," and "sudden turns of sarcastic wit," and the *Overland Monthly* agreed it contained "some of the most noteworthy verse of the sort that has been published for years in this country." The *Pacific Ensign,* west coast organ of the W.C.T.U., solemnly accorded Stetson a place among the "brightest poets," and Henry Norman in the *London Daily Chronicle* celebrated her "vigorous verse" which breathed "the spirit of humanitarian progress."[15] As Stetson observed in her diary for 4 February 1894, "My little book is going off spendidly. . . . Splendid reviews of it, appreciative personal letters, orders from individuals, telegram for fifty copies from Woman's Journal; general enthusiasm. I must have a new edition."[16] In 1895, a British publisher, T. Fisher Unwin, issued a reprint of the first edition. A Scottish paper declared it "one of the most engaging volumes of modern poetry we have come across" and the *London Saturday Review* reprinted from it the poem "A Conservative," the sardonic parable of a butterfly newly emerged from his chrysalis and utterly dismayed by his unexpected and irresistible metamorphosis:

> "I do not want to fly," said he,
>   "I only want to squirm!"
> And he drooped his wings dejectedly,
>   But still his voice was firm:
> "I do not want to be a fly!
>   I want to be a worm!"
>   (*ITOW,* 100–101)

When, the next year, Stetson visited England, she found that she enjoyed a greater reputation there "than at home, based on the little book of poems" (*L,* 201). A second American edition of *In This Our World,* with 122 poems on 184 pages, also appeared in 1895; and a third edition, with 149 poems on 217 pages, in 1898.

The reviews of these later editions were almost unanimously favorable. John Bonner concluded in the *San Francisco Wave*, with no hint of irony, that Stetson was "one of the poets of the age, standing side by side with Bret Harte."[17] Her literary agent Henry Austin plugged "the 'ultra-barbaric yawp' of this California Apostle of the New Woman" in the *Bookman*, and William Morton Payne asserted in the *Dial* that a "note of indignant passion . . . thrills through the poems in Mrs. Stetson's volume."[18] According to reviewers for *Literature* and *Current Literature*, respectively, Stetson had struck "a really new note" in the volume and displayed a "vigor, 'verve,' deep moral earnestness, and delightful humor and extraordinary talent for satire which . . . have hardly been surpassed."[19] Her friend Charles Lummis of *Land of Sunshine*, the author of *A Tramp Across the Continent*, pronounced the poetry "remarkable," though "less lyric or dramatic than polemic and brilliant," and the poet "easily the satirist of her day."[20] To be sure, as if to arm her critics, Stetson disclaimed any poetic pretention. The lyrics in *In This Our World* were, in her opinion, no more worthy of the tag "literature" than her heavy-handed, didactic stories. As she told an interviewer in 1896, "I don't call it a book of poems. I call it a tool box. It was written to drive nails with."[21] Literary editors such as Harry Thurston Peck leapt at the chance to damn with faint and chauvinistic praise: Stetson "stands head and shoulders above any of the other minor poets of her sex," Peck averred. "In fact, did we not know the author's name, we should have selected many of the poems collected in this volume as having been written by a man."[22] ("Read Peck's review," Stetson sniffed in her diary: "Very poor wit.")[23] Similarly, Helen A. Clarke in *Poet-lore* criticized Stetson's heterodox themes and stilted versification and concluded she "is not a lyrist by nature."[24] But, as if to contradict this assertion, a reviewer for the *London Athenaeum* claimed a few months later that some of Stetson's lyrics "are perfect of their kind. There is a firm and certain touch about them which betrays unmistakably the hand of the born artist."[25]

The chorus of praise for *In This Our World* is all the more surprising in light of Stetson's increasingly irregular scansion and informal style of verse. Before 1890, she usually wrote verse with regular meter and rhyme, especially sonnets and rondeaux. After 1890, however, she often wrote free verse modeled after Whitman. When, in 1883, William O'Connor offered her a copy of *Leaves of Grass*, she had been "obliged to decline" the gift, as she noted in her diary, "as

I had promised Walter I would not read it."[26] However, in a lecture written in February 1891, soon after the Stetsons permanently separated, she hailed Whitman as "America's greatest poet" and quoted his entire poem "Beginners."[27] In another lecture two weeks later, she quoted section 32 of "Song of Myself" and, in her diary for 10 August 1891, she mentioned reading *Leaves of Grass* for pleasure.[28] She also alluded to Whitman in her agrarian-satirical poem "Their Grass," written in May 1897.[29] Like Whitman in successive editions of *Leaves,* moreover, Stetson dropped and added poems and reordered their sequence until settling, in the third edition of *In This Our World,* upon the form she preferred. The poem "Birth," for example, does not appear at all in the first edition, appears on page 153 of the second edition, and significantly enough opens the third edition on a note of celebration:

> Lord, I am born!
> I have built me a body
> Whose ways are all open,
> Whose currents run free
> *(ITOW,* 1)

For a period of two years in the late 1890s, during which time she lived literally out of a trunk, she carried with her on tour but two books: Schreiner's *Dreams* and Whitman's *Leaves of Grass.*[30] Her publishers Small and Maynard gave her another copy of *Leaves* the day they accepted for publication the manuscript of *Women and Economics,* and she read from it to Houghton Gilman, who fortunately "liked it too."[31]

Occasionally, Stetson's poetry betrayed Whitman's influence in more subtle ways. In "The Dalliance of Eagles," for example, he had described

> The rushing amorous contact high in space together,
> The clinching interlocking claws, a living, fierce, gyrating wheel,
> Four beating wings, two beaks, a swirling mass tight grappling,
> In tumbling turning clustering loops, straight downward falling.

The eagles then soar upward in "their separate diverse flight, / She hers, he his, pursuing." In "Wedded Bliss," Stetson rewrote Whitman's poem from a feminist perspective:

"O come and be my mate!" said the Eagle to the Hen;
   "I love to soar, but then
   I want my mate to rest
   Forever in the nest!"
   Said the hen, "I cannot fly,
   I have no wish to try,
But I joy to see my mate careering through the sky!"
They wed, and cried, "Ah, this is Love, my own!"
And the Hen sat, the Eagle soared, alone.
                                    (*ITOW*, 157)

Stetson has, in a word, revised Whitman, sacrificing his music and erotic imagery to her ironic point of view. She often quoted Whitman's verse in her later work, subsequently joined the Whitman Society of New York, and, as late as 1921, proclaimed publicly that the memory "of Walt Whitman will live."[32]

Not surprisingly, Horace Traubel, the St. Paul of the Whitmaniacs, defended her art in an early review of *In This Our World*. He addressed the "critics of the press and of parlors" who "do not think Mrs. Stetson a poet," and his comments merit quotation at length:[33]

Read Birth, an opening door. Read The Lion Path, and courage will come easier to you. Read Heroism, and you will spiral your way to the summit of moral intuition. Read Part of the Battle and tighten your armor. Read The Modern Skeleton and partake of no more feasts till all may be fed. Read Wings. If you are a minor poet you will not wonder more why your poetry is minor. Here is a touch light as The Skylark's. Read Among the Gods. You will never again dare to accuse her of want of phrase, though her phrase is not cited in handbooks on versification. Read Motherhood, read Mother to Child. Woman never wrote so to woman before—never in such quick demand or passionate service. Then read all the poems in the final section, The March, especially The Wolf at the Door, and Hardly a Pleasure, the last powerfully dramatic in its contrasts. If you can maintain any prejudice against Charlotte Stetson's art after you have done as much as this I should be more than astonished. You have met a woman with no indecent reticences who sings because singing becomes her sentiment. Forgive yourself possible prejudices and hereafter talk less about rules of art and a little more about its substance.

Stetson was exceptionally pleased by this review, which Traubel showed her in advance of its publication.[34] Later, she also submitted two original poems to Traubel for publication in the *Conservator*.

W. D. Howells was a no less enthusiastic champion of Stetson's verse. Like a belletristic sentry, Howells stood watch from his editorial perch to hail the first sign of approaching talent. In 1891, during his short-lived tenure with *Cosmopolitan,* he solicited from her a contribution, "something as good and 'wicked' as 'Similar Cases.' "[35] In 1894, after Stetson presented him with a first edition of her verse anthology, Howells wrote her to express the "pleasure we have all taken in your book of poems. They are the wittiest and nicest things that have been written this many a long day and year. . . . I rejoice in your gift fearfully, and wonder how much more you will do with it. I can see how far and long you have thought about the things at hand; [though] I have my bourgeois moments when I could have wished you for success's sake to have been less frank. But of course you know that you stand in your own way! The thing can be done."[36] Howells subsequently echoed these comments publicly in both *Harper's Weekly* in 1896 and the venerable *North American Review* in 1899: "Mrs. Charlotte Perkins Stetson has made a place of her own," he declared. "Her civic satire is of a form which she has herself invented; it recalls the work of no one else." Indeed, "since the Biglow Papers we had no civic satire, that I can think of, nearly so good," at least "no satire approaching it in the wit flashing from profound conviction." Still, "the implications of her satire are for social reform of a very radical kind" and so, fortunately or not, "I am afraid that the acceptance of Mrs. Stetson's satire is mostly confined to fanatics, philanthropists and other Dangerous Persons. But that need not keep us from owning its brilliancy."[37] Stetson first met Howells in person at the Single Tax Club in New York in March 1897 and, over the years, they often socialized. One memorable day in December 1897, in fact, she introduced Howells to Jane Addams, the progressive reformer and founder of the settlement-house movement in Chicago, and listened while "they talk[ed] about Tolstoi. Miss A. had a message from him to Mr. H."[38] As late as 1911, Howells wrote the poet with the news that he had reread "Similar Cases," found his original enthusiasm for it unabated, and "shared the joy of it" with his daughter Mildred. "When the gods really wake up and begin to behave justly you will have no cause to complain," he added.[39] On her part, Stetson appreciated Howells's patronage. "He didn't wait for others anywhere or for more books, he reached out a strong hand at the first word. I'll never forget it," she wrote Houghton Gilman. It was his "nature to carp at accepted masters and to dare speak at once to the unrecognized new author. I think very highly of him for more than personal reasons."[40] Though her reputation would grow over the years, Stetson would gain renown not as a poet, as Howells thought, but as a lecturer and social theorist.

"At Large"

During her tenure as editor of the *Impress,* Charlotte Perkins Stetson established wide contacts within the woman's movement. She helped to organize several annual Woman's Congresses, convened at Golden Gate Hall in San Francisco under the auspices of the PCWPA, which assembled "the foremost women of the state, showed what progress was being made, and introduced noted speakers from the east." Harriet Howe recalled forty years later that "There was never anything to compare with those Women's Congresses, at least on the Pacific Coast, either before or since."[41] The Congress of May 1895, convened shortly after the magazine suspended publication, was especially noteworthy: Stetson met Anna Howard Shaw, Susan B. Anthony, the grand dame of the suffragists, and Jane Addams, a "truly great woman" whose "mind had more 'floor space' in it than any other I have known" (*L,* 184). Anthony tried to enlist Stetson in the suffrage campaign, and Addams became her "champion" and urged her to visit Hull House. She accepted the latter invitation with alacrity. Her work in California closed in the summer of 1895. "I had put in five years of most earnest work, with voice and pen, and registered complete failure," she later recalled. At the age of thirty-five, she considered her life a "failure, a repeated, cumulative failure" (*L,* 176). She borrowed money, pulled up stakes, and caught a train for Chicago. Thereafter she would be less a nova in the literary firmament than a sociologist. She would continue to compose poetry and fiction, but she would no longer presume to earn either a competence or a reputation as an imaginative writer.

For the next five years, she claimed no permanent residence. She visited and lectured "from California to Maine, from Michigan to Texas, from Georgia to Oregon, twice to England." Over the years, she was impressed less by the rigidity of the social status quo than by the opportunities to reform it. "What I saw in the world was not its foolish, unnecessary troubles," she wrote, "but its splendid possibilities" (*L,* 182–83). During a three-month stay in Chicago, Stetson met "distinguished people, humanitarian thinkers from all over the country, and from other countries, too." Her "verse was known and liked" there, and soon she began to lecture once more. She was impressed by "the advanced condition of sociological study and social enthusiasm" in the city, inspired by "Miss Jane Addams and others" and "embodied in the *Journal of Sociology* and the scientific work of such men as Professor [Thorstein] Veblen of C[hicago] University."[42] Although, for reasons of health, she declined an invitation to head a settlement house in Little Hell on the North Side, she recommended Helen Campbell for the post "and helped as I could with the work, still lecturing as opportunity offered" on such topics as child culture, the economic independence and specialization of women, and her "organic theory of social economics," later elaborated in *Human Work*. Her intellectual sphere rotated on an axis whose poles were suffrage and socialism. "I worked for Equal Suffrage when opportunity offered," as she explained, "believing it to be reasonable and necessary, though by no means as important as some of its protagonists held; and for Socialism, feeling the real basis of that system to be right, in spite of the mishandling of Marx" (*L,* 186–87).

She carried her convictions to a national forum for the first time in January 1896, when she attended the twenty-eighth annual Women's Suffrage Convention in Washington, D.C. She preached there on "The Spiritual Significance of Democracy and Woman's Relation to It" and addressed the House Judiciary Committee hearings on a suffrage amendment. In a speech to the delegates on "The Ballot as an Improver of Motherhood," she argued, with "good success,"[43] that the vote was not an end in itself but merely one means of realizing a larger goal: "The suffrage draws the woman out of her purely personal relations and puts her in relations with her kind, and it broadens her intelligence. . . . A woman will no longer be attached solely to one little group, but will be also a member of the community." Like the "unnatural mother" of her story, a woman with a vote will be impelled to widen her perspective beyond the narrow confines of the home and to consider larger questions of social import. Stetson also endorsed in debate Elizabeth Cady Stanton's *Woman's Bible,* a commentary which analyzed how scripture discriminated against women, and she read selections of her verse, including her chestnut "Mother to Child":

> Thou art one with the rest. I must love thee in them.
> Thou wilt sin with the rest; and thy mother must stem
> The world's sin. Thou wilt weep; and thy mother must dry
> The tears of the world lest her darling should cry.
>   I will do it—God helping!

And I stand not alone. I will gather a band
Of all loving mothers from land unto land.
Our children are part of the world! do ye hear?
They are one with the world—we must hold them all dear!
Love all for the child's sake!

For the sake of my child I must hasten to save
All the children on earth from the jail and the grave.
For so, and so only, I lighten the share
Of the pain of the world that my darling must bear—
Even so, and so only!

                                                                (*ITOW*, 142)

The poem was received "with great applause"[44] and, over the years,
it "proved especially efficacious in bridging the gulf which generally
exists between personal and social motherhood."[45] In all, as a reporter
for the *Woman's Journal* concluded, "Those of us who have for years
admired Mrs. Stetson's remarkably bright poems were delighted to
meet her."[46]

The convention in Washington was, in Stetson's opinion, propi-
tious for other reasons both personal and intellectual. There she first
met Lester Ward, the leading Reform Darwinist in America. In his
pioneering sociological treatises, Ward advocated a variety of reforms,
including state intervention in the marketplace and equal rights for
women, by "correctly rereading" Darwin. In effect, Ward argued
that, because the human animal possesses a mind, this beneficiary of
"telic" evolution is not subject to the same brutal struggle for existence that obtains among the lower orders. There is no exact analogy,
such as Herbert Spencer assumed, between the biological organism
and the social organization. Instead, humans acting in concert,
through government, can direct the subsequent course of evolution
by manipulating their environment. According to Ward, humans are
active agents charged with the task of planning their corporate des-
tiny, not ruthless competitors whose personal survival is determined
by unalterable traits and conditions. Humanity is the master, not the
subject, of indifferent nature. Ward thus rationalized from evolutionary premises a basis for socialized commonwealth, not accumulated
personal wealth. In arguing for social action, he disposed of the doctrine of determinism which anchored Spencerian social ethics. Ward
also argued, *contra* Darwin, that the female is the true and original
"race-type" and the male the "sex-type"—that is, that the female is

the original form of a species and the male merely assists in the process of fertilization. Unfortunately, the "gynaecocentric" or female-dominant prehistoric culture had been superseded in the modern age by "androcentric" or male-dominant gender hierarchy. Thus he concluded, once more on evolutionary premises, that sexual selection or choice of a mate is properly a female prerogative and that nurturant females possess traits of altruism which favorably distinguish them from naturally aggressive males: "While the voice of nature speaking to the male in the form of an intense appetitive interest, says to him: fecundate! it gives to the female a different command, and says: discriminate! The order to the male is: cross the strains! that to the female is: choose the best!"[47]

Stetson had followed Ward's career for years before they met. In 1889, she clipped an article about his work that had appeared in the *Woman's Journal* and, in the spring of 1893, one of her poems appeared on the same page of the *New Nation* as one of his essays.[48] A year later, she described Ward in the *Impress* as "a great man, a clear, strong, daring thinker, and one whose style of writing is easy to the uninitiated yet satisfying to the learned."[49] She doubtless referred to Ward's seminal essay "Our Better Halves" (1888) in which, as she asserted in *Women and Economics,* he "clearly [proved] the biological supremacy of the female sex" (*W&E,* 171) a half-century before Ashley Montagu. Ward had written that "Woman is the unchanging trunk of the great genealogic tree; while man, with all his vaunted superiority, is but a branch, a grafted scion, as it were, whose acquired qualities die with the individual, while those of woman are handed on to futurity. Woman *is* the race, and the race can be raised up only as she is raised up. . . . True science teaches that the elevation of woman is the only sure road to the evolution of man."[50] Women are the transmitters of those traits, both inherited and acquired, which guarantee progress. Unfortunately, men have usurped the natural prerogatives of women. To continue to skew the process of sexual selection and to deny women opportunities to exercise their creative talents is tantamount to race-suicide. Later, when the Wisconsin sociologist Edward A. Ross asked Charlotte Perkins Gilman to list the sources which most influenced the writing of *Women and Economics,* she cited only two, one of them this essay by Ward (*L,* 259).

Ward initiated their acquaintance several weeks before the suffrage convention when he wrote Stetson to request a copy of *In This Our World.* He soon afterwards wrote her again to express both his ad-

miration for her poetry and the hope he might arrange a reception in
her honor while they were together in Washington. Ward and Stetson were introduced on 23 January 1896, the first day of the convention, and the reception he hosted for her occurred as scheduled on 28
January.[51] Years later, she still recalled one of her first impressions of
"this great soul." Delegates to the convention had discussed questions
worn smooth by debate when Ward "rose to his feet, a towering figure, tall, broad, massive, with a noble head, and a face that wore the
kindness of large wisdom. He admitted the value of the local measures, the temporary palliatives which had been offered, but in adding
his suggestion said: 'I confess that nothing deeply interests me in social improvement which does not apply to the whole human race.' "[52]

The anecdote is illuminating, for Stetson was immeasurably impressed by Ward and by his perspective on the human condition. He
was "quite the greatest man I have ever known," she later wrote. "He
was an outstanding leader in Sociology, familiar with many sciences,"
and his gynaecocentric theory of sexual differentiation, she thought,
was "the most important contribution ever made to 'the woman question,' " perhaps even "the greatest single contribution to the world's
thought since Evolution" (L, 187). Though she never purported to
grasp the import of his entire oeuvre, she believed that, if only on
the basis of this theory, best elaborated in chapter 14 of *Pure Sociology*
(1903), "he should stand as the greatest light ever thrown upon
[women's] abnormal condition." All of Stetson's later work would re-
sound with Ward's ideas, and she would specifically dedicate to him
"with reverent love and gratitude" her treatise *The Man-Made World*
(1911), her most systematic popularization of the gynaecocentric theory. In a black-bordered obituary in the *Forerunner*, Charlotte Perkins
Gilman eulogized her friend and mentor upon his death in 1913: "He
has taught us to understand and relate the facts of social life; he has
pointed out to us our line of march, our best steps upward."[53] As late
as 1933, she declared that "Whitman and Ward are our two greatest
Americans."[54]

After the close of the suffrage convention in Washington, as her
celebrity widened, Stetson spent more of her time on the hustings.
Between 2 January and 3 July 1896, she delivered at least fifty-seven
sermons and addresses, an average of over two per week, on such topics as dress, motherhood, and suffrage in locales as far east as cosmopolitan Boston and as far west as provincial Eureka, Kansas
(L, 190). On 8 July, she left Chicago for England to attend the Inter-

national Socialist and Labor Congress, registering as a delegate of the Alameda County Federation of Trades. At the meetings and a peace demonstration in Hyde Park she gravitated into the orbit of the Fabian Society, a "group of intelligent, scientific, practical and efficient English Socialists" who rejected class revolution in favor of social-democratic legislation and whose rolls included the names of Beatrice and Sidney Webb, the future British prime minister Ramsay MacDonald, and George Bernard Shaw (*L*, 203). In their company she spurned the Marxists and derided the Anarchists, though she thought Prince Kropotkin at least "interesting,"[55] and, to her delight, she was soon invited to join their ranks. Over the next four months she traveled throughout England reading her poetry and preaching from the tail of a socialist van,[56] met William Morris and Alfred Russel Wallace, and wrote an article for the *Progressive Review*. She also composed some wretched verse for American publication which might serve as a textbook example of the pathetic fallacy:

> Wet winds that flap the sodden leaves!
> Wet leaves that drop and fall!
> Unhappy, leafless trees the wind bereaves!
> Poor trees and small!
>
> *(ITOW*, 91)

She also met the socialist Edward Carpenter, who fashioned for her a pair of leather sandals that she proudly showed Howells later[57] and that were "still in working order" when she wrote her autobiography in the mid-1920s (*L*, 203).

Stetson's affiliation with the Fabians continued long after her return to the States. On 10 December, according to her diary, she agreed to become a regular contributor to the monthly *American Fabian*. Eugene Hough, her old friend from California days, introduced her to readers with the observation that oppressed workers "know and love and appreciate" her, "their ablest, bravest, and most unselfish friend and leader." Over the ensuing months, she wrote a series of dramatic "classes in sociology" in which a teacher of socialism engages in dialogue with such figures as a politician, a millionaire, a manufacturer, and a scientist. The teacher reconciles competition and individualism, for example, by arguing that we must "erect cooperative industries on the wish for individual gain" and, in the fourth lesson, s/he explains the advantages of "kitchenless homes." In addition, Stetson contributed to the magazine a number of miscellaneous essays (e.g., "Selfishness and Socialism," "When Socialism Began") and occasional poems, such as "His Own Labor," a strident denunciation of surplus value:[58]

> Let every man be given what he earns!
> We cry; and call it justice. Let him have
> The product of his labor—and no more!

Stetson also attended meetings of the Fabian Study Club in New York. At the meeting of 9 May 1897, in particular, she befriended Henry Demarest Lloyd, author of the antimonopoly tract *Wealth against Commonwealth* (1894), a favorable review of which she had published in the *Impress*.[59] " This man was a seer, a social diagnostician, almost a prophet," she later wrote.[60] Stetson even recited to the assembly her old Nationalist lyric "Similar Cases."[61] In all, the Fabians were a catalyst to her own intellectual ferment during these months.

She decided at last to strike out on a new project: an essay about the economic basis of sexual oppression. On 1 July 1897, she recorded in her diary that she had got "hold of a new branch of my theory, the biggest since I saw it. Now I can write the book."[62] Three weeks later, she discussed "the big new idea" with Jane Addams, who was "really impressed. To have her see it is a great help."[63] Though she did not stipulate the idea in her diary, it was probably a cousin to one she recorded later: "The sense of duty is developed in proportion to our specialization. Ethics only *conscious physics.*"[64] Even as she retreated from creative literature, she began to invoke scientific or mechanistic metaphors in her analyses of human conduct. "My method was to approach a difficulty as if it was a problem in physics, trying to invent the best solution," she wrote. "Here was Law, at last," indeed "laws that could be counted on and *Proved.* That was my delight, to know surely" (*L*, 61, 29). Ethics is but "the physics of social relation," she later asserted (*CC*, 97, 105; *MMW*, 126). In October 1897, she was compelled to discourage "talk of my taking the editorship" of the *American Fabian* "for $25 a month,"[65] for she was by then deep into the first draft of her most important and most characteristic work, tentatively entitled *Sex in Social Economics.*[66]

Women and Economics

Charlotte Perkins Stetson's essay on "the economic factor between men and women as a factor in social evolution" was the culmination of the feminist and socialist critique she had formulated over the previous decade. It actually contained little that was new to her work. "After years of thinking," she explained in her autobiography, "I now set to work on my first book, in prose, named by the publishers *Women and Economics*" (*L*, 235). Like Veblen in *The Theory of the Leisure Class* (1899), Stetson argued that sexual oppression originated in prehistoric times when men, rather than competing naturally for mates, exercised their superior strength to subjugate women and appropriate their domestic labor. Much as Marx rationalized capitalism as a way-station on the road to socialism, Stetson excused patriarchy as a pre-industrial stage of social organization once necessary for the preservation of the species but now obsolete. Though women were the trunk and men but the branches of the genetic tree, women were forced in primitive times to depend upon men for basic necessities. "We are the only animal species in which the female depends on the male for food, the only animal species in which the sex-relation is also an economic relation," as she noted (*W&E*, 5). Moreover, she disputed the prevailing opinion that motherhood disqualifies a woman for work outside the home. In a later lecture, in fact, she paralleled the plight of an economically dependent mother with "the case of the she-hornbill, who, while in her nest, is all walled in by mud, with only her big beak protruding; and into this the he-hornbill puts the food to sustain her."[67]

Thus men and women became unequal partners in a simple economic transaction—food and shelter in exchange for domestic servitude—and the relationship was sanctified by church and state and reinforced through millennia. "The sexuo-economic relation," as she referred to it, "began in primeval savagery. It exists in all nations. Each boy and girl is born into it, trained into it, and has to live in it" (*W&E*, 79). As a result of the environmental obstacles to equality, woman is, at present, but a social parasite or, at best, a domestic animal, a type of horse which enables man to produce more wealth more efficiently or a type of milk-cow whose sexual attributes are overdeveloped (*W&E*, 13, 44). However, the traditional division of labor along sexual lines is not ordained by nature. To enhance their value to men, women have become oversexed—that is, to the detriment of the race, they have accentuated and commercialized sexual characteristics and adapted to subordinate sex-roles in order to attract and keep mates. "We are not better as parents, nor better as people, for our existing degree of sex-distinction, but visibly worse," as Stetson concluded (*W&E,* 34). Excessively feminine, insufficiently human, women marry for money, not love. Men postpone marriage until they are "established"—that is, until they earn enough money to impress their wives. Predictably enough, meanwhile, prostitution flourishes in the barbaric marketplace where sex is a bartered commodity: "We have produced a certain percentage of females with inordinate sex-tendencies and inordinate greed for material gain. We have produced a certain percentage of males with inordinate sex-tendencies and a cheerful willingness to pay for their gratification" (*W&E,* 96).

Fortunately, the relation between men and women may be purged of its sexuoeconomic character. Increasing numbers of women have exploited opportunities to become economically independent, partly because the women's movement, including such organizations as the W.C.T.U. and local women's clubs, has challenged traditional limits and pressed for reform. "The change considered in these pages is not one merely to be prophesied and recommended," Stetson observed, for "it is already taking place under the forces of social evolution" (*W&E,* 122). She expressed confidence that, as these forces are harnessed, as women's work becomes more specialized, "a newer, better form of sex-relation and of economic relation" will evolve (*W&E,* 142). Thus the woman's movement "should be hailed by every right-thinking, far-seeing man and woman" as we march "toward economic equality and freedom" (*W&E,* 144). The standard of progress is not the number of states granting women the vote but "the changes legal and social, mental and physical, which mark the advance of the mother of the world toward her full place" (*W&E,* 148). "Day by day the bars go down," she declared in the polemical style of the pamphleteer. "More and more the field lies open for the mind of woman to glean all it can" (*W&E,* 149). The 1890 census counted three million American women at work outside the home.

In the second half of the tract, Stetson outlined her more heretical notions and justified her refusal to genuflect at the altar of the matriolatry cult. Maternity is no more sacrosanct than other occupations, she averred, and is no less amenable to specialization. Indeed, "the more absolutely woman is segregated to sex-functions only, cut off from all economic use and made wholly dependent on the sex-relation as means of livelihood, the more pathological does her motherhood become" (*W&E,* 182). Rather than the "guileless manoeuvres" the woman now learns to attract a provider-protector, she should be instructed in her duties as mother of the race. Undoubtedly, the trend toward the economic independence of women will prompt changes in "the home and family relation. But, if that change is for the advantage of individual and race, we need not fear it" (*W&E,* 210). Stetson took no direct issue with monogamy or the marriage institution per se, asserting instead that the marriage relation will improve when women no longer depend on their husbands for their livelihood. More particularly, she again called for the creation of a class of professional housekeepers and food-preparers whose services might be individually purchased. She explained the allied advantages of the kitchenless house. She called for child-care centers or kindergartens staffed by trained specialists so that, among other benefits, a mother might work for wages outside the home rather than spending the accumulating energies of the race in her small cage" (*W&E,* 257). In fine,

We are not going to lose our homes nor our families, nor any of the sweetness and happiness that go with them. But we are going to lose our kitchens, as we have lost our laundries and bakeries. The cook-stove will follow the loom and wheel, the wool-carder and shears. We shall have homes that are places to live in and love in, to rest in and play in, to be alone in and to be together in; and they will not be confused and declassed by admixture with any industry whatever. . . . To free an entire half of humanity from an artificial position; to release vast natural forces from a strained and clumsy combination, and set them free to work smoothly and easily as they were intended to work; to introduce conditions that will change humanity from within, making for better motherhood and fatherhood, better babyhood and childhood, better food, better homes, better society,—this is to work for human improvement along natural lines. . . . And it is already happening. All we need do is to understand and help. (*W&E,* 267–68, 317)

The entry of large numbers of women into the labor force would even purge the marketplace of its "brutal ferocity of excessive male energy" (*W&E,* 113) and, willy-nilly, spell the end to capitalism: "We shall live in a world of men and women humanly related, as well as sexually related, working together, as they were meant to do, for the common good of all" (W&E, 313). Thus Stetson opined, in a tone unfailingly optimistic.

Unfortunately, she seems not to have considered seriously the plight of women and mothers forced to work for wages. Economic independence, from her middle-class perspective, meant a profession, a career, the opportunity to earn a reputation, and, as I. M. Rubinow of the U.S. Bureau of Labor noted as early as 1909, "the possibility of transferring the drudgery of the home upon other shoulders." However, Rubinow added, "To the working class woman it means none of these desirable things. It may mean very long hours, unhygienic work, low wages. . . . For this very good reason the workingwoman, the workingman's wife, refuses to grow enthusiastic over the middle-class ideal of economic independence."[68] In 1890, over half of the women employed in jobs outside agriculture were domestic servants, most of them recent immigrants or black, and fewer than 10 percent were professionals. In 1910, about 40 percent of women employed outside agriculture were servants and only about 12 percent professionals.[69] Stetson failed to win mass support for her ideas in her own day because, simply enough, she appealed to too narrow a constituency.

She composed the first draft of Women and Economics in barely five weeks during the summer and early autumn of 1897. She wrote as many as four thousand words per day, and completed a manuscript of some 35,600 words, less than half the length of the finished version, on 8 October. She recorded in her diary with some relief on 12 October that Houghton Gilman had "read it—likes it—says its good."[70] Within a month, she had contracted with Small, Maynard & Co. of Boston to issue both the essay and a new edition of In This Our World. She submitted the final draft of Women and Economics in January 1898 and the book appeared for sale on 1 May.[71] Despite its crude style, she harbored great, even grandiose expectations of it: "I think that the thing I am here to do is a big thing—the truths I see [are] deep basic truths, and that I have been given unusual powers of expression," she wrote her cousin three weeks after the date of publication, "and I truly hope that my life will count for much good in the world—as Darwin's did and Galileo's and many another blessed soul who was given high place to serve the world."[72]

The book was exceptionally well-received by professional women and literary reviewers. Jane Addams and Florence Kelley, the founder of the National Consumer League, called Women and Economics, respectively, "a Masterpiece" and "the first real, substantial contribution made by a woman to the science of economics."[73] It was adopted as a textbook at Vassar College and it was read by, among others, Charmian Kittredge, the future wife and biographer of Jack London.[74] Moreover, according to Stetson, "the reviews were surprising, numerous, respectful" (*L, 270*). Emma Ireland hailed the treatise in the New York *Nation* as "the most significant utterance on the subject [of sexual oppression] since Mill's 'Subjection of Women.' "[75] (Stetson noted in her diary that this was a "Fine review.")[76] Charles Lummis indulged his penchant for florid metaphor by describing it in the *Land of Sunshine* as a "most extraordinary book, a book which will never be dropped out of the reckoning so long as its problem is a problem, an enduring meteor in the sky, a flaming sword which wise enemies will shrink from."[77] Helena Born in the *Conservator* pronounced Stetson's analysis "masterly."[78] Mabel Hurd of Columbia University expressed reservations in the *Political Science Quarterly* about her method, but agreed that Stetson's Fabian perspective on the sexuoeconomic relation was fresh and provocative and that as a result "her book will be widely read and discussed, as the cleverest, fairest and most forcible presentation of the views" of feminists generally.[79] Arthur Woodford described the work in the *Dial* as "profound social philosophy" stated "with enough wit and sarcasm" to make it "very entertaining reading."[80] In her review in the *North American Review*, Violet Paget ("Vernon Lee") commended "the originality, the scientific soundness and moral efficacy" of *Women and Economics* and testified that she was converted to the feminist cause by it.[81] Small and Maynard authorized a British edition and, as Stetson later noted, "The book was warmly received in London, with long, respectful reviews in the papers" (*L, 260*). The *London Daily Chronicle*, for example, declared that since Mill's essay "no book dealing with the whole position of women has approached" Stetson's study "in originality of conception and brilliancy of exposition,"[82] and the London *Bookman* acknowledged her "exceptional ability" and "great courage."[83] Favorable reviews also appeared in, among other publications, the *New York Times*, the *Independent*, the *Brooklyn Eagle*, the *Boston Advertiser* and *Transcript*, the *Sewanee Review*, *Current Literature*, the *Humanitarian*, the *Southern Educational Journal*, and the *Westminster Gazette*. The work was subsequently translated into German, Dutch, Italian, Hungarian, Japanese, French, and Russian, and passed through seven editions in English by 1911. "It sold and sold and sold for about twenty-five years," Stetson later observed (*L*, 270), with total sales in the tens of thousands. As a result of *Women and Economics*, Carl Degler concluded, Stetson "became the leading intellectual in the woman's movement in the United States during the first two decades of the twentieth century."[84] T. V. Smith declared in 1927 that the study was "not only one of the great classics on women's rights but a rich mine of insight on social relations in general."[85]

With the publication of *Women and Economics*, Stetson was able finally to pay old debts she had incurred during her residence in California. She was established as a writer, and on the basis of her literary reputation the imperious owner and editor of *Cosmopolitan*, John Brisben Walker, eagerly solicited her work. Walker "wants me to send him all I write," she noted in her diary in April 1899. A few days later, Walker asked her "to take a salary and work for him."[86] She briefly considered the offer but, after visiting his office "and observing how he treated his editors, I declined" (*L*, 256). Fortunately, she could afford the luxury of refusal. By the time she attended the International Congress of Women in London in late June and early July 1899,[87] she was an international celebrity. Those broad themes she discussed comprehensively in *Women and Economics* she would treat in fuller detail in dozens of articles and four major sociological treatises written over the next dozen years.

Chapter Three
The Major Phase

Charlotte Perkins Stetson enjoyed public acclaim during the decade of the 1890s but, especially during her years as an itinerant lecturer, she endured occasional bouts of loneliness and depression. During a trip to England, for example, she logged a revealing note in her diary: "Find that I am really low again. O dear! It is so lonely. Try to write something on social evolution to rest my brain."[1] She recognized, if implicitly, that she had sacrificed personal intimacy to her work. To be sure, the trade-off between emotional fulfillment and career ideals was not absolute. Such contemporary feminist leaders as Elizabeth Cady Stanton and Carrie Chapman Catt had reconciled marriage and social activism, but after her divorce Stetson harbored "no faintest intention of ever marrying again" (L, 284).

However, she changed her plans. In 1897, she renewed her acquaintance with a cousin, Houghton Gilman, a patent attorney in New York, and soon they agreed to wed. Whereas her marriage to Walter Stetson had been complicated by the birth of a daughter and the fear of subsequent pregnancy, she welcomed sexual partnership when she thought she had passed child-bearing age. Sex without the threat of pregnancy seemed to her, as she wrote, a "Happy thought—take no precautions—take no treatment—all runs smoothly and nothing happens!!!"[2] Over the next three years, Stetson traveled the lecture circuit much of the time and, in her letters, covenanted with her future husband. They agreed that, after marriage, both would continue to pursue careers. Should she be forced to choose between him and her work, Stetson warned, "two hearts might break and I might die of the breaking, but I could not choose other than one way." In the letters they exchanged, they negotiated the terms of their union. She insisted that they "work out such a plan of living as should leave me free to move as move I must." She wished to practice economic independence: "I *must not* focus on home 'duties'; and entangle myself in them. Remember it is not an external problem with me—a mere matter of material labor and time. However vague and absurd my talk may seem to you, it is practical enough to be a question of life

57

and death to me."³ After they were married in a "very short and reasonable service" in Detroit in June 1900,⁴ they rented an apartment in New York and boarded nearby. Katharine joined them in July. As Charlotte Perkins Gilman wrote in her memoirs, "Here was home at last, a very pleasant one, the best of husbands, and at last my daughter—I was very happy" (*L*, 283–84). Thus she began her most productive period. "How beautifully I can hurl every idol from the shrine," she wrote Houghton Gilman, when "I myself am living in blissful content in a small flat with you."⁵ Over the years, he attended her lectures, accompanied her to club meetings, helped with her research, read her writings, and generally sympathized with her perspective on questions of social import. Occasionally they disagreed. Charlotte Perkins Gilman observed in her diary in November 1902, for example, that she had "Tried to argue with Ho[ughton] on social organism & [got] very tired." A few weeks later, she noted with "great happiness" that "He begins to admit [my] main position."⁶ Through thirty-four years of marriage, however, Houghton Gilman remained essentially a bystander rather than a participant in the movements which engaged her imagination.

In the story "Three Women," published in *Success* in 1908, Gilman reflected on her decision to remarry. The protagonist, Aline Morrow, a kindergarten teacher, receives a proposal of marriage from a prominent physician. Her mother, who had sacrificed a promising musical career to marry, counsels Aline to spurn the offer and continue to teach. Her aunt, who once declined a proposal because she preferred to paint, urges her to marry and resign her position at the school. Aline heeds neither recommendation. She agrees to marry the physician on the condition that she may be "your wife—I could be a mother—and a teacher too." They arrange to hire house-service by the hour and to order their meals from a caterer. The resolution reflects the one the Gilmans reached in fact. The tale ends on a sentimental note as the lovers embrace.⁷

In her heyday, Charlotte Perkins Gilman was a popular and prolific speaker and writer, a respected authority on issues as narrow as the housefly menace and as trivial as public gum-chewing, and as broad and weighty as race and war. In 1904, she briefly joined the staff of the *Woman's Journal* as a contributing editor. In June 1904, she addressed the International Congress of Women in Berlin and, the following year, she lectured on tour through England, Holland, Germany, Austria, and Hungary.⁸ When H. G. Wells visited the

U.S. in 1906, he specifically sought out Gilman, though they apparently "did not hit it off personally."[9] Afterwards, she complained that "Wells loses his perspective and clear vision when he considers women. He sees women as females—and does not see that they are human." His "masculine limitations" are "marked and persistent."[10] Over the years, too, Gilman cut a familiar figure at suffrage meetings in New Orleans, Washington, D.C., Portland, Oregon, and other cities,[11] and, from 1899 to 1910, she was a regular contributor to such major magazines as the *Saturday Evening Post, Harper's Bazar,* the *Independent, Appleton's, Scribner's, Success,* the *Delineator,* and *Woman's Home Companion.* Meanwhile, she wrote book-length treatises entitled *Concerning Children* (1900), *The Home* (1903), *Human Work* (1904), and *The Man-Made World* (1910), as well as a novel, *What Diantha Did* (1910), and occasional stories and poems, variations on themes she addressed in her nonfiction. For example, in late 1904 she formed a plan, later abandoned, to write "an Epic Poem on Womanhood" ending with the inauguration of "the New Day of *Freedom and Right Union.*"[12] Throughout the works she composed during this major phase of her career, Gilman intertwined four intellectual threads—the economic emancipation of women through specialization and remunerative work, a social motherhood featuring experts in child-care, socialized housekeeping and the kitchenless home, and the gynaecocentric theory of sexual differentiation.

Specialization and Human Work

In the spring of 1899, shortly before leaving for the London Congress, Stetson began an essay on assignment from *Cosmopolitan*[13] in which she defined work as the social function for which the individual is specially fitted. The two essential features of work, she asserted, are mutualism, or labor for the common good, and specialization, or increasing division of labor. In the organic community of human animals, as in the beehive or anthill, one's "individual interest is best served by his serving the interests of others" and "the common interest is best served by an increasing specialization in labor."[14] This essay, "What Work Is," might serve as an outline to *Human Work,* the sequel to *Women and Economics* that she hoped would capitalize on its success. In the fall of 1899, shortly after returning from the London Congress, she negotiated a lucrative contract with Small and Maynard to publish a "piece of social philosophy, as to the nature of human life and its economic processes" (L, 275), that she planned to complete in the course of the winter. In December she moved to a boarding house near Pasadena and, in March 1900, Charles Lummis reported that expectations ran high, at least "among those whose expectancy counts for anything," in "whatsoever book it is" that she was writing "outdoors on a breezy foothill of the Sierra Madre overlooking one of the fairest and most Bostonized valleys in the world."[15]

Unfortunately, ambition was not equal to execution in this instance. The treatise *Human Work* would not appear until 1904, after interminable revisions and postponements. The essay "was not to be reeled off like my usual stuff," as Gilman explained in her autobiography, for

> Here was an enormous change of thought, altering the relationships of all sociological knowledge. As in astronomy we had to change from the geocentric to the solar-centric theory of our planetary system, with complete revision of earlier ideas, so here was a change from the ego-centric to the socio-centric system of sociology, with wide resultant alterations in prior concepts. Furthermore, it was a treatise so large in scope as to cover all human life, and in the four times I did it over I never knew where to begin. (L, 285)

The book was eventually issued not by Small, Maynard & Co. of Boston, who had contracted for it, but by McClure, Phillips & Co. of New York, who agreed to pay royalties to the author only "after a certain number were sold." In the end, she "got nothing from it" (L, 286). It was, as she later reflected, at once "the greatest book I have ever done, and the poorest—that is, the least adequately done" (L, 275). She again revised it for serialization in the *Forerunner* between 1912 and 1914 under the titles "Our Brains and What Ails Them," "Humanness," and "Social Ethics," but that version "was worse" than the last. In 1932, shortly before her death, she made another attempt to systematize her theory in a twenty-two chapter typescript entitled "A Study in Ethics" left among her papers. With sublime confidence bordering on arrogance, she considered her social ethics as advanced and as recondite a system as Einstein's physics,[16] though she finally abandoned the project to "later thinkers [who] must make it plain" (L, 286).

The treatise has lamentably few of the virtues of Gilman's earlier work. Whereas *Women and Economics* builds analytically to a conclusion, *Human Work* is poorly organized, ponderous, redundant, and discursive. In the opening chapters, Gilman diagnosed the social pathology in familiar, if florid, terms. "Our most conspicuous troubles to-day are economic," not religious or political, she asserted (*HW*, 12). Moreover, the root of our economic evil is an overwrought individualism which breeds morbid self-interest and sanctions cutthroat competition and sexuoeconomic inequalities. Gilman viewed society holistically, as an organic form of life, an integration of component parts like the human body with the welfare of each part dependent on the welfare of the whole. She elsewhere expressed her disdain for the social status quo by burlesquing in hackneyed verse Alexander Pope's injunction in "An Essay on Man" that "Whatever is, is right":[17]

> Whatever is we only know
> As in our minds we find it so;
>   No staring fact is half so clear
>   As one dim, preconceived idea—
> No matter how the fact may glow.
> . . . .
> Our ancient myths in solid row
> Stand up—we simply have to go
>   And choke each fiction old and dear
>   Before the modest facts appear;
> Then we may grasp, reluctant, slow,
>   Whatever is.

Among the "myths" Gilman exploded were the "Pay concept" and the "Want theory"—the notions, respectively, that people must be threatened with punishment or bribed with reward before they will work, and that if their personal desires were otherwise gratified they would choose not to work. According to Gilman, echoing Lester Ward, human animals in an advanced stage of "telic" or intellectual evolution, joined in organic community, often are motivated by self-sacrifice and in turn exempted from the savage struggle for existence. Despite the forces of social inertia, "To-day we are rapidly approaching a social organism limited only by the earth," she prophesied (*HW*, 100). Every person who devotes his or her life to social service, performing productive tasks among friends, "may be as calmly happy as any browsing cow, as ecstatically happy as any soaring lark" (*HW*, 108). Thus specialized workers such as sailors and miners, even soldiers in the ranks, are more cooperative than farmers, asocial atavists who purport to self-sufficiency.

At length, in chapter 9, near the midpoint of the book, Gilman stated her thesis. She defined work as "an expenditure of energy by Society in the fulfilment of its organic functions. It is performed by highly specialized individuals under press of social energy, and is to them an end in itself, a condition of their existence and their highest joy and duty" (HW, 182). She appealed for a cosmic perspective on work and an identification with the group, as in her poem "Eternal Me":18

> What an exceeding rest 'twill be
> When I can leave off being Me!
> To think of it!—at last be rid
> Of all the things I ever did!
> Done with the varying distress
> Of retroactive consciousness!
> Set free to feel the joy unknown
> Of Life and Love beyond my own!
> . . . .
> But Heaven! Rest and Power and Peace
> Must surely mean the soul's release
> From this small labeled entity—
> This passing limitation—Me!

Charles Lummis observed in the Land of Sunshine that, as the final two lines of this poem illustrate, "I do not know anyone else whatever who can put so much into so few, so simple, words."19

Gilman gave her analysis a feminist turn by discussing work as an extension of the maternal role in nature. Woman is a procreator and a nurturer, thus "to work and save is feminine" whereas the "fighting and grabbing attitude comes from primitive animal egoism, a low rudimentary condition, and the morbid overplus of sex-energy in the male" (HW, 207–8, 217). Like Bellamy, who proposed an "industrial army" to rationalize production, Gilman endorsed industrial organization on a military model.20 She welcomed technological innovation as a boon to productivity and dismissed the potential for worker alienation from the product of labor with the glib assertion that "the normal human being can not only sustain extreme specialisation, but glory in it" (HW, 235). Similarly, she opined that unskilled labor such as washing clothes may represent "high social service and social sacrifice" (*HW,* 245). As Dolores Hayden observes, because Gilman "was relatively uncritical of 'good business' practices under capitalism, her proposals promised to subject women to the hierarchy and alienation of wage work under capitalism as the price for ending their physical isolation and economic dependence."[21]

Gilman extended her analysis to indict the foibles of the outmoded "leisure class." Much as the robber barons like John D. Rockefeller and Andrew Carnegie receive wealth far in excess of their contribution to society, the economic elite consumes conspicuously, according to pecuniary canons of taste, with "meretricious display and cultivated wastefulness which form another phase of our abnormal consumption" (*HW,* 309). Here Gilman followed the lead of Thorstein Veblen, whose "valuable, interesting, and occasionally delightful work" on the leisure class she first read in early 1900. She had been introduced to Veblen personally during a visit to Chicago later that year and found him an "Interesting man." She later averred that Veblen had "irrefutably" explained the persistence of primitive attitudes among the higher circles.[22] She added that women are especially susceptible to the problem of superabundant leisure. The parasitic role assigned to them exacerbates the tendency to inordinate and gross consumption. Gilman cited examples from Shakespeare and Zola: "Cleopatra outdid Anthony in 'conspicuous consumption'—swallowing a dissolved pearl worth more than all his gobbled delicacies" and "Nana destroyed expensive furnishings just to amuse herself" (*HW,* 315). The society columns of newspapers, obsequious reports of dances, dinners, and dresses, have value only as symptoms of the social pathology. Fortunately, the leisure class "can be eliminated by healthy action on the part of the real social body" by such means as the redistribution of wealth through progressive taxation, the rigorous operation of sexual selection to improve the stock, and the realization of sexuoeconomic equality. Like government of the people, the leisure class "has no existence except as we make and uphold it" (*HW,* 347).

Reviews of *Human Work* were decidedly mixed. On the one hand, Mary K. Ford suggested in *Current Literature* that the work was "original, forceful, and stimulating, whether or not her ideas commend themselves to our reason."[23] The Boston *Literary World* pronounced it "a subtle and thorough analysis"of economic processes and the *Brooklyn Eagle* rhapsodized, with surprising ebullience, that there "is not a dull page in this book." The *San Francisco Star* concluded that with the essay Gilman "places herself among the foremost students and elucidators of the problem of social economics," and the *Chicago Tribune* hailed the volume as "the best thing that Mrs. Gilman had done." On the other hand, the *Chicago Post* carped that the treatise "does not contain a single original idea. It does contain much crude, shallow, fallacious, loose writing." The *Kansas City Star* similarly complained about Gilman's "irresponsible versatility" in manipulating data to her advantage.[24] H. W. Boynton deplored Gilman's methodological peccadillos: "An impatient habit of generalization compromises the effectiveness of the book both from the literary point of view and as a scientific study."[25] More ambiguously, the *Boston Transcript* granted the perspicacity of Gilman's analysis but insisted that she failed to "suggest a practical course of action applicable to the present time."[26] In her memoirs, Gilman admitted she was both pleased and disappointed by the study. She claimed that "its theories, if accepted, and better carried out by later thinkers, will completely alter the base of our economic science, and so our conduct." However, she acknowledged, "So far it has made practically no impression" (*L,* 275). Despite the mixed reception of *Human Work,* Gilman did not publicly question her own special genius, her function as a catalyst to social reform. As she wrote in the treatise, "Again and again we see the whole race seized and pushed on by some dominant individual life, the currents of whose action vibrate unceasingly through the mass, and stir it to better growth" (*HW,* 31). She might have been commenting on her own argument for social motherhood and her critique of the traditional home.

Social Motherhood

By the summer of 1900, Charlotte Perkins Gilman was obliged to lay aside the manuscript of *Human Work* in order to write "something shorter" which would fulfill the terms of her contract with Small and Maynard (*L,* 281). Her next published book, written in the course of a few weeks and issued in December in a first edition of two thousand copies, was dedicated to daughter Katharine and entitled *Concerning Children.*

Like *Human Work,* this treatise was little more than an inflated magazine piece. Gilman admitted in her diary that it was "not very good stuff."[27] She predicated her argument on the obsolete Lamarckian theory that parents transmit acquired characteristics to their offspring. According to this theory, the transmission of acquired characteristics over several generations would produce progressively greater intelligence and strength in the heirs. In other words, Gilman repudiated the more modern scientific view, popularized in the late-nineteenth century by August Weismann, that parents determine the traits of their children genetically within limits liable to mathematical calculation. As she wrote, "The way to make people better is to have them born better. The way to have them born better is to make all possible improvement in the individual before parentage," especially during "the precious ten" years between the ages of fifteen and twenty-five.[28]

Lamentably, Gilman embraced a biology that reinforced racism and blatant nativism. If a child may inherit the parents' acquired traits, then a child born into an "advanced" civilization is *ipso facto* superior to a child born into a "backward" culture. Or, as Gilman explained, "If you were buying babies, investing in young human stock as you would in colts or calves, for the value of the beast, a sturdy English baby would be worth more than an equally vigorous young Fuegian. With the same training and care, you could develop higher faculties in the English specimen than in the Fuegian specimen, because it was better bred" (*CC*, 4). Surprisingly, for one inclined to puncture other cultural stereotypes, Gilman shared popular preconceptions about racial attributes, especially those of Jews and blacks (cf. *HW*, 128; *L*, 245). Later, she even endorsed the eugenics movement and the objective of "race-improvement" through birth control, including sterilization of the "unfit."[29]

However ill-informed her science, Gilman's Lamarckian views fortunately do not discredit her appeal for progressive child-culture. The plasticity of human nature allows the individual to be improved indefinitely, whether or not that improvement is transmissible. In the subsequent chapters of *Concerning Children,* Gilman elaborated her doctrine of environmental reform. Training a child to strict obedience, she argued, "has a bad effect on the growing mind," for such training "does not develop the brain, but checks its growth" (*CC*, 37, 41). Though she addressed the problem in the third person, she outlined her own predicament when she attained her majority:

A girl is twenty-one. She has been properly reared by her mother, whom we will suppose to be a widow. Being twenty-one, the girl is old enough to begin to live her own life, and naturally wishes to. . . .

"Not so," says her mother. "Your duty is to stay with me. I need you."
Now the mother is not bed-ridden. She is, we will say, an able-bodied
woman of forty-five or fifty. . . . The daughter prefers to go to New York,
and study music or art or dressmaking, whatever she is fit for. But here is
her dear mother claiming her presence at home as a duty. (CC, 162–63)

Thus Gilman at once excused her own adolescent rebellion against an
overbearing mother and obliquely attributed her later emotional tur-
moil to her enforced obedience as a child. Doubtless recalling her an-
guish of the mid-1880s, she reflected on the "struggles of the
dethroned mind to get possession of its own body again, as the young
man or woman grows to personal freedom." As she knew from personal experience, "It takes years of conscientious work to re-establish
the original line of smooth connection [between thought and action],
and the mended place is never so strong as it would have been if it
had not been broken" (CC, 60–62). In addition, she again expressed
her xenophobic views: "Those races where the children are most absolutely subservient, as with the Chinese and the Hindu, where parents are fairly worshiped and blindly obeyed, are not races of free
and progressive thought and healthy activity." On the other hand,
"our American children, who get less of the old-fashioned discipline,
make better citizens than the more submissive races who were kept
severely down in youth, and are unable to keep themselves down in
later life" (CC, 55, 89). Gilman concluded that a child should learn
discipline experientially by touching the hot stove, for example,
rather than retiring under threat of corporal punishment. The
mother, in particular, should teach her children "by example as well
as by description" and, if she cannot, "she should provide a teacher
more competent" (CC, 116). At this point in her analysis in a later
lecture, she would tell of a "model mother" who refused to suffer the
annoyance of her own children before they reached the age of ten. So
she entrusted them to a "sister next door," much as Gilman had sent
Katharine to Grace Channing for five years, meanwhile "visiting
them, bringing them gifts, and speaking cheerfully to them" until
they were older. Then she "took them home and mothered them herself," and as a result "there grew up between them a warm and abid-
ing love that might otherwise have been destroyed by grinding
friction."[30]
    Gilman turned in the latter half of her essay to her concept of "so-
cial motherhood." Because mothers are rarely trained to be teachers,
she explained, infants are normally at the mercy of amateurs inexpe-

rienced in their duties. The cult of domesticity and the idealization of motherhood hinder women from discharging their larger social duties. Gilman refused to genuflect at the altar of household gods and dismissed the matriolatry implicit in celebrations of the maternal instinct. Predictably, antifeminists accused her of striking at the roots of the family, even of advocating free love and other blasphemies,[31] but she simply argued that child culture should be entrusted to specialists, teachers at "baby-gardens" and kindergartens, even as adolescents are sent to school and college. "Perhaps, if mothers could command such assistance as this," she once declared, "motherhood would not be dreaded and avoided as it is now, and our beloved President [Theodore Roosevelt] would not be so afraid of the suicide of the American race."[32] Gilman believed most of these experts would be female for, as she asserted, "The care of children is certainly the duty of women" (*CC,* 155). The professional child-specialist exemplifies the role Gilman expected women to fill in a socialized economy. She later insisted that "The great Specialist in Child Culture should be as highly honored and paid as a college president" and that "Child Culture is a work of immeasurable importance. It calls for Special Talent, Thorough Training, and Long Experience."[33] If professional child care is unavailable for any reason, she proposed that groups of perhaps six mothers form a cooperative whereby each of them supervises all of the children one day per week, freeing each of them in turn to perform remunerative work on the other days. What seemed strange and radically innovative to many early readers now seems normal and commonplace. Gilman also gave an ironic twist to the phrase "unnatural mother." If doting parents are "natural," she suggested, better are the "unnatural" ones: "The unnatural mother, who is possessed of enough intelligence and knowledge to recognize her own deficiencies, gladly intrusts her children to superior care for part of the time, and constantly learns by it herself." The unnatural mother refuses to be a house-servant and nurse-maid, but arranges her household "on a basis of organised professional service, with skilled labour by the hour, and so has time to perform some professional service herself, and pay well for the better performance of the 'domestic' tasks." Whereas the natural mother cares only for her own children, the "unnatural mother cares for Children,—all of them" (*CC,* 274–77). "Social parents" shoulder responsibility for children in general much as, on a smaller scale, taxpayers fund public education.

Reviews of *Concerning Children,* while few in number, were generally favorable. The *New York Times* praised Gilman's "original and illuminating thoughts" on the subject and concluded her volume deserved "a large and heedful public."[34] Similarly, the *New York Press* opined that it "should be read by every mother in the land."[35] Oscar Lovell Triggs, in *Unity,* commended the author for her "keen analysis and sound philosophy,"[36] and Florence Winterburn, in *Charities,* agreed the book represented "an excellent addition to sociological literature," though she added Gilman's prose suffered from "a certain pomposity and, at times, considerable obscurity."[37] A dissenting note was sounded by the *Athenaeum,* whose reviewer complained that Gilman's generalizations about the "educational requirements [of children are] strangely deficient in judgment and common sense."[38] Despite the paucity of publicity, sales of the book were brisk. A second edition of two thousand copies was issued in February 1901 and the work was subsequently translated into Dutch (*L,* 301).

Gilman addressed the question of social motherhood again in later works. For example, in a 1907 tract, *Women and Social Service,* she summarized her earlier analysis and concluded that "It is not sufficient for a child to have his own mother. A child needs to have, in addition to his mother, social parentage."[39] In other essays, she endorsed the educational reforms of Pestalozzi and Fröbel and particularly applauded the increasing popularity of Montessori schools. "For the immeasurable value of her work and its direct application to humaniculture," she wrote, "we should give love and honor to this latest of the great Italians, Dr. Montessori."[40] Similarly, in her story "A Garden of Babies" (1909) she portrayed a young woman who, in modern parlance, supervises a day-care center. Trained as a nurse and teacher, the woman began to care for children when her husband and child died unexpectedly. Over the years, she has built a reputation for integrity: "She doesn't treat a baby like a doll-idol—or a Teddy bear!" the narrator observes. "She respects it. There is reverence in her love—and understanding." The advantages of her scientific day-nursery are readily apparent. Children in her care are healthier and happier than children exclusively in their mothers' care. The infant mortality rate has declined. Women are less apprehensive about bearing children if they anticipate professional assistance in raising them. The director of this laboratory day-care has even trained other qualified women who open similar centers.[41] In "Making a Change" (1911), Gilman portrayed a young mother who grows so despondent she attempts suicide, at which point her "very capable" and "affectionate" mother-in-law steps in and opens a "baby-garden" on the upper floor and roof of their building. "Mother showed me the way out," the young woman explains to her ever-so-practical husband, "the way to have my mind again—and not lose you!" (*CPGR*, 66–74). Though the stories fail aesthetically, like most fiction designed to prove an ideological point, they concretely illustrate the doctrine of social motherhood and depict baby-gardens as eminently practical alternatives to traditional modes of parenting.

Socialized Housekeeping

"What I want to see people get rid of," Charlotte Perkins Gilman declared in a public lecture in March 1903, "is the idea that home is sacred because the dinner is cooked there. Home is sacred because love and congeniality and companionship are there."[42] The stove is neither an altar nor a throne. Though she has been scorned as an eloquent if misguided critic of the family, Gilman limited her attack to the single-family home, an institution she considered inherently dirty, inefficient, and repressive. She had often essayed the subject in brief since 1893, as in "The Domestic Cookshop," published in *Worthington's Illustrated* in July 1893, "The Home Without a Kitchen" in the *Puritan* for December 1899, and "Homes Without Housekeeping" in the *Delineator* for May 1907. "The center of difficulty in the home is the kitchen," she wrote. "In it and its irregular functioning lies the main source of the expense of housekeeping, the labor of housekeeping, the dirt, disease, difficulty, worry, uncertainty, and general unpleasantness incident to housekeeping."[43] Gilman published a coherent and comprehensive diagnosis of the problem under the title *The Home: Its Work and Influence* in late 1903. She long considered this work "the most heretical—and the most amusing—of anything I've done" (*L*, 286), and at least one modern historian has pronounced it "a *tour de force*, in its own way more impressive than *Women and Economics*."[44]

From the outset, Gilman contended that the purpose of her work was "to maintain and improve the home," not abolish or dismantle it in "iconoclastic frenzy" (*H*, 3, 18). The home "*in its essential nature* is pure good," she asserted, though it had failed to evolve at the same rate as other institutions "and by its rudimentary condition it arrests development in other lines" (*H*, 8, 10). "The home is the cradle of all the virtues," she suggested, "but we are in a stage of social development where we need virtues beyond the cradle size" (*H*, 183). The ostensibly "modern" home is, in effect, a "relic of the harem."[45] Gilman's analysis frequently echoed, on a higher frequency, points she had made in *Women and Economics,* as when she traced the origin of the home to the prehistoric expropriation of the domestic labor of women.

Gilman built her case against the home on the pillars of economics and sociology. The modern home, as she portrayed it, is a model of disorganization which oppresses women. At present, families who "keep house" merely maintain a private commissary, dormitory, laundry, and nursery. These home industries may be amenable to more scientific management, as her friend Helen Campbell had demonstrated over the years, but they remain intrinsic to the institution as we know it. "We are founding chairs of Household Science, we are writing books on Domestic Economics; we are striving mightily to elevate the standard of home industry," she wrote, yet "we omit to notice that it is just because it is home industry that all this trouble is necessary" (*H,* 93). The woman working at a low industrial level in the home must perforce ignore her larger civic responsibilities, and the conditions of home life cramp her perspective and limit her intellectual growth. The woman who "lives always in a small dark place, is always guarded, protected, directed, and restrained, will become inevitably narrowed and weakened by it. The woman is narrowed by the home and the man is narrowed by the woman" (*H,* 277). The race can progress only so far as woman raises her station. The impediments she faces are structural, not sexual. Whereas the man enjoys advantages of specialized work outside the home, the woman suffers the corresponding disadvantages of unspecialized domestic industries. She is willing to work; indeed, she "works harder and longer than the man, in a miscellaneous shifting field of effort far more exhausting to vitality than his specialised line; *and she bears children too!"* (*H,* 291).

Gilman reserved especial criticism for the industries incident to food preparation. The kitchen and the "home-cooked meal" are no more sacrosanct than the nursery and the home-bred child, she averred. The preparation of meals, like the culture of children, should be entrusted to specialists. Much as home-spun clothes and home-baked bread have been rendered obsolete by modern garment mills and bakeries, the private kitchen will disappear beneath the rising tide of the central kitchen or "food laboratory," or so she thought. "We pay rent for twenty kitchens where one kitchen would do," Gilman estimated. If communities of kitchenless homes were organized by city-block or apartment building, thirty chefs might replace the two hundred women who cook individual meals for their families. If economies of scale were fully exploited, the cost of meals might be reduced by two thirds and, with the emancipation of wives, the labor force and family income would increase by nearly one half.

Such a neat division of labor made nutritional as well as economic sense. Specialists in food-preparation would both recognize adulterated meats and milk and enjoy the clout necessary to abolish them from the marketplace. "The purchase of food in quantities by trained buyers would lift the grade of our supplies at once," she explained. "No man is going to waste time and money in adulteration subject to daily analysis, or in offering stale, inferior articles which will not appear saleable to the trained eye."[46] She illustrated the advantages of her system by reference to public bakeries: "Our American baker's bread has risen greatly in excellence as we make less and less at home. All the initial processes of the food supply have been professionalised" (*H,* 331). With improved nutrition, moreover, Gilman anticipated the imminent disappearance of the saloon for, as she explained, "insufficient and ill-chosen food, villainously cooked, is one great cause of man's need for stimulants" (*H,* 294). She was unusually sanguine, perhaps, but at least she recognized the dimensions of the problem. Later, in the midst of the adulterated meat scandal, Gilman joined her satirical voice to the clamor for reform:[47]

> The American public is patient,
> The American public is slow,
> The American public will stand as much
> As any public I know.
> We submit to be killed by our railroads,
> We submit to be fooled by our press,
> We can stand as much Government scandal
> As any folks going, I guess.
> We can bear bad air in the subway,
> We can bear quick death in the street,
> But we are a little particular
> About the food we eat.
> It is not so much that it kills us—
> We are used to being killed;
> But we like to know what fills us
> When we pay for being filled.

When we pay the Beef Trust prices—
As we must, or go without—
It is not that we grudge the money,
But we grudge the horrid doubt.
Is it ham or trichinosis?
Can a label command belief?
Is it pork we have purchased, or poison?
Is it tuberculosis or beef?

Charlotte Perkins Gilman silhouetted the problem of adulterated food in *The Home* several months before Upton Sinclair began to write his exposé of the Chicago stockyards. However, Gilman and Sinclair proposed distinctly different regimens of treatment, and the contrast helps to explain Gilman's failure to inspire large-scale reform. Whereas she pressed for the professionalization of housekeeping, Sinclair propagandized for socialism and precipitated, however inadvertently, passage of the Pure Food and Drug Act and government inspection of foodstuffs susceptible to spoilage. Whereas Gilman failed to gauge accurately the attachment of most Americans to the single-family home, Sinclair heralded the welfare state. Gilman's essay was designed to persuade individuals to improve their habits. She hoped to effect change by example rather than by law. Sinclair's novel sparked public outrage and immediate political action. Even Gilman later wrote him to express "a real belief in your genius; and an admiration for some of your work."[48] At the risk of oversimplification, Gilman embraced a utopian solution to the problem of contaminated foods and Sinclair spurred practical reform. Years later, she still faulted attempts "to improve the quality of our food supplies" by "federal laws" and "local inspections," for "no one seems to see that the one permanent continuing cause of poor food is the helplessness of the private purchaser."[49]

In the crux of the essay, Gilman called for a "new order of duties, a new scale of virtues" which would putatively transform the home from workshop to retreat (*H*, 313).

Set the woman on her own feet, as a free, intelligent, able human being, quite capable of putting into the world more than she takes out, of being a producer as well as a consumer. Put these poor antiquated "domestic industries" into the archives of past history; and let efficient modern industries take their place, doing far more work, far better work, far cheaper work in their stead.

In the new order, everyone will be better fed, clothed, and educated. The man will enjoy "a strong, free, stimulating companion all through life" and also "will be able to work to far better purpose in the social service." The "man and woman together" will be both "relieved of most of their personal cares" and "better able to appreciate large social needs and to meet them" (*H*, 321–22). Gilman reassured her readers she wished neither to separate mother and child nor to destroy the family institution. Not only will the kitchenless home prove a boon to women with careers, she suggested, it will allow "the smooth and rapid development of a higher type of marriage," "a more satisfying matrimony,"[50] a more egalitarian monogamy.

Gilman was careful to distinguish the kitchenless homes of her proposal from communal kitchens or cooperative housekeeping. She formed the conclusion early, after she joined a communal group with her mother in the spring of 1874, that "Cooperative housekeeping is inherently doomed to failure" (*L*, 26). Not only are people in such circumstances too often tempted to shirk their share of the household duties, but they are normally even less qualified to discharge them than the typical wife and mother. That is, according to Gilman, cooperative housekeeping fails because it mistakenly presumes "a capacity in families for common responsibility and common action." The cooperator "expects persons who have made a failure of keeping house alone to succeed in keeping house together!" But groups of families contain no more specialized workers than individual families: "Whereas the very essence of the trouble lies in the inefficiency of the unspecialized workers, most cooperative colonies consist of persons less capable in this line rather than more."[51] Make no mistake: "I have always been outspokenly against every form of household cooperation."[52] Still, despite her protestations, Gilman's proposal to professionalize and socialize housework was often labeled a cooperative scheme.

By all accounts, *The Home* was both widely reviewed and critically acclaimed. Gilman saved dozens of these reviews among her papers. Such journals as the *Washington Post,* the *Boston Transcript,* the *Chicago Tribune,* the *New York Tribune,* and the *New York Times* punctuated their notices with the adjectives "bright," "brilliant," "original," "remarkable," "incisive," "interesting," and only occasionally "vituperative."[53] In the *Critic,* Olivia H. Dunbar described the study as "a surgical operation on the popular mind" which succeeds "in shattering practically all the domestic furniture now in use" in a tone of "genial satire."[54] To be sure, such reviewers as Mary K. Ford in *Current Literature* and Edith Granger in the *Dial* protested that women of child-bearing age were unable to compete with men in business and the professions: "The rush is so great, the struggle so keen, that it takes all of a man's strength to keep up; how is a woman to do so?" Thus, in their view, Gilman's plan to reorganize the home was vain and purposeless, in spite of its originality.[55] On the whole, however, Gilman's analysis was well-received. Sinclair praised Gilman by name in chapter 30 of *The Jungle* (1906), though Gilman later protested that he misunderstood her proposals (*L,* 26). The study was translated into German and a second American edition appeared in 1911. Walter Lippmann commended Gilman's work on domestic economy in *Drift and Mastery* (1914),[56] and Charles and Mary Beard in *The Rise of American Civilization* (1928) credited her theories with inspiring "a new school of feminist thinkers" in America and Europe "which sent reverberations as far afield as awakening Japan."[57]

As in *Women and Economics,* Gilman pitched her analysis in *The Home* to appeal to the emerging class of professional women who could afford to hire domestic help. Rather than a radical reordering of domestic priorities, as Dolores Hayden explains, Gilman's program was in may ways "a belated and conservative expression" of concern about "the consequences of industrialization and urbanization" on the home. The apartment hotel was, in her portrayal, "an ideal environment for the respectable, monogamous married couple, just as it was an ideal business venture for the female capitalist, and offered an ideal managerial position for the professional domestic economist."[58] Who exactly would do the drudge-work? Gilman replied, with an air of bourgeoise superiority, those "who liked to do such work" (*W&E,* 247) or who were "most fitted" for it (*H,* 319). In effect, professional women might purchase their independence from the home at the expense of others, usually women. The scientific day-nursery she proposed in *Concerning Children* required a professional staff, but a central kitchen or laundry still required mostly menial labor.[59] As Hayden concludes, "Gilman failed to develop a sufficiently complex analysis of the ways in which class position modified women's experience of domestic work."[60] She failed to view the problem from the perspective of the cooks and laundresses hired under her plan.

Gilman at first seemed to correct this oversight in her first complete novel, *What Diantha Did,* serialized in the *Forerunner* in 1909–10 and soon after issued privately by the Charlton (*Charl*otte +

Hough*ton*) Company. The enterprising twenty-one-year-old heroine
Diantha Bell resigns her teaching position and leaves her middle-class
family to settle in bucolic Orchardina, a small town in southern California, where she becomes a perfect servant and housekeeper. However, Gilman soon betrayed her class bias. With the help of Viva
Weatherstone, a maternalistic capitalist sympathetic to her schemes,
Diantha soon establishes a restaurant, a cooked food delivery, a cleaning service, a cluster of kitchenless homes, and an apartment hotel.
She operates all of them according to sound business practices and
opens her account books to any reader who wishes to audit them.
"You know what I'm after—to get 'housework' on a business basis,
that's all," Diantha tells her mother, "and prove, *prove*, PROVE what
a good business it is."[61] She displays admirable managerial skills, at
least from the perspective of conservative economists. She pays loyal
employees slightly higher wages than they might earn as live-in do-
mestics, protects them from sexual harassment, and even organizes a
company House Workers Union. "*What Diantha Did* leaves no doubt
about the economic basis of Gilman's domestic reforms," Hayden
concludes. "She is a romantic advocate of benevolent capitalism," despite her profession of Fabian socialism.[62] Rather than a proletarian
novel like *The Jungle*, *What Diantha Did* traces the protagonist's rise
from maid to manager. Because Gilman subordinated story to theme,
most early reviewers justly complained that the novel limped pro-
nouncedly on the episodic plot-leg. Lilian Brandt complained in *Survey* that the story "has slight merit,"[63] and the reviewer for the
Independent described it as a "statistical romance" rather than a
novel.[64] Upon the publication of a British edition, the *London Academy* allowed that had Gilman's "book been concerned merely with a
story, we should have found it dull."[65] Fortunately, Gilman serialized
another work concurrently in the *Forerunner* which was better
received.

The Gynaecocentric Theory

In *The Man-Made World* (1911), Gilman proposed to detail "the
effect upon our human development of this unprecedented dominance
of the male," the sex-type, and the aborted development of woman,
the race-type (*MMW*, 6). She emphasized for the first time hereditary
versus environmental factors as influences on character. Like Lester
Ward, she granted in her analysis innate differences between the

sexes: "The basic feminine impulse is to gather, to put together, to construct; the basic masculine impulse to scatter, to disseminate, to destroy" (*MMW*, 114). Women are naturally laborious, men combative. Like Ward, too, she distinguished between merely sexual characteristics and human traits shared in common by both sexes: "Every handicraft, every profession, every science, every art, all normal amusements and recreations, all government, education, religion; the whole living world of human achievement: all this is human. That one sex should have monopolized all human activities, called them 'man's work,' and managed them as such, is what is meant by the phrase 'Androcentric Culture' " (*MMW*, 25). Unfortunately, our androcentric culture reverses the natural order. During the matriarchate, the prehistoric era of female dominance, men competed for women who exercised the prerogative of sexual selection. Now, however, men exercise sexual selection, often choosing the weakest women. Thus "the woman was deprived of the beneficent action of natural selection, and the man was then by his own act freed from the stern but elevating effect of sexual selection. Nothing was required of the woman by natural selection save such capacity as should please her master; nothing was required of the man by sexual selection save power to take by force, or buy, a woman" (*MMW*, 52). During the matriarchate, the woman nurtured the children, "the father being her assistant in the great work." When the family became patriarchal and proprietary, however, the woman and children were confined to the home. As Gilman noted, "The whole enginery of the family was turned from its true use to this new one, hitherto unknown, the service of the adult male" (*MMW*, 32–33). Of course, she also traced a current of historical progress. During the matriarchate, ethical values "depended for sanction on a cult of promiscuous but efficient maternity" (*MMW*, 131). The higher ethical standards of monogamy and fidelity evolved, however imperfectly, during the patriarchate. Fortunately, the process of social evolution promises a "nobler type of family," a union of man, woman, and child which will "promote our general social progress" (*MMW*, 43).

Gilman organized the remainder of the treatise according to the same principle, focusing in each chapter on a particular human habit or institution perverted by androcentrism. Most of her analysis now seems less advanced than familiar, testimony to the accuracy of her prognosis and breadth of social critique.

Dress. Clothing becomes functional through the force of right natural selection and beautiful through right sexual selection, but "under a too strictly inter-masculine environment" men wear a "mainly useful but beautiless costume" and women heed absurd precepts of fashion and ornamentation (*MMW*, 61).

Art. Similarly, art and especially literature have been "masculized": "Fiction, under our androcentric culture, has not given any true picture of woman's life, very little of human life, and a disproportioned section of man's life." Most novels fall into one of two categories, adventure stories about men struggling with other men or with natural elements or love stories about men passionately chasing women. Similarly, most poetry is but the ceaseless outcry of the male for the female. To be sure, there are rare and welcome exceptions to this rule, such as Balzac's and Dickens's novels and *Uncle Tom's Cabin* (*MMW*, 100, 102, 104). However, the humanizing of women opens new fields to writers of fiction—e.g., the resolute woman who refuses to leave her career to marry, the middle-aged wife who realizes at last "that her discontent is social starvation," and the interaction of women with women and mothers with children (*MMW*, 105).

Play. We also discriminate between male and female games and sports, for example, by giving the boy models of boats, trains, and doctor kits while giving the girl dolls and tea sets. Lamentably, Gilman added, "It has not yet occurred to us that this is monstrous" (*MMW*, 110–11).

Religion. All modern faiths express male canons of belief. The oldest religions revered goddesses of motherhood and service, but "under masculine dominance Isis and Ashteroth dwindle away to an alluring Aphrodite" (*MMW*, 138). The Manichean heresy is characteristic of the masculine mind which, Gilman explained, cannot conceive of a "God without an Adversary" (*MMW*, 139). The same "masculine instincts" color "masculine ethics," the sexual double standard the most notorious example (*MMW*, 134).

Education. Because most men believe that women belong in the home, women have suffered sexual discrimination in their attempts to receive equal educational opportunities: "Under this androcentric prejudice, the equal extension of education to women was opposed at every step, and is still opposed by many. Seeing in women only sex, and not humanness, they would confine her exclusively to feminine interests" (*MMW*, 147). However, Gilman predicted, "the time is coming" when women will be as well educated as men and they "will recognize the educative possibilities of early childhood." We will then see "a development of the most valuable human qualities in our children's minds such as would now seem wildly Utopian" (*MMW*, 162).

Government and Law. Whereas the matriarchate was organized along "maternal lines of common love and service," the patriarchate is organized for predatory purposes, specifically to hunt and to wage war (*MMW*, 179). The "inextricable masculinity" of government so conceived "revolts at the idea of women as voters," hence the resistance to the suffrage movement (*MMW*, 187). Full political enfranchisement of women, however, "would mean care, nurture, provision, education" (*MMW*, 189–90). As in Bellamy's Boston, crime would be treated in hospitals (*MMW*, 203), and international disputes resolved by diplomacy, not war.

Economics. The cut-throat competition that now characterizes the economic marketplace is but a modern form of sex-combat among males. This rudiment of primitivism "introduced into business has been a discordant jarring note all through our civilization."[66] However, both the feminist and labor movements, "parts of the same pressure, the same world-progress" (*MMW*, 260), are gradually correcting economic injustices. When women, who lack the instinct for sex-combat, are full participants in the business of the world, economic competition will be replaced by the principle of mutual service (*MMW*, 238).

"We have progressed thus far," Gilman concluded, "in spite of and not because of our androcentric culture" (*MMW*, 243). She did not call for a retrogression to gynaecocentric culture, but for equality between the sexes: "The advance of civilization calls for human qualities, in both men and women" (*MMW*, 155). However, like a coiled mainspring ready for release, long-restrained womanhood would speed the evolutionary steps upward: "The distinctly feminine or maternal impulses are far more nearly in line with human progress than those of the male" (*MMW*, 235). She refused to predict "what, if any distinctions there will be in the free human work for men and women, until we have seen generation after generation grow up under absolutely equal conditions" (*MMW*, 250). As a new world dawns, we accelerate our progress toward economic democracy and free womanhood.

Gilman readily conceded the influence of Lester Ward and his gy-naecocentric theory on her work. In the spring of 1897, to be sure, she admitted privately to Houghton Gilman that she planned to read Ward's *Dynamic Sociology* (1883) and *Psychic Factors of Civilization* (1893) "when my head is equal to it," though she had skimmed "his chapters that touch women."[67] In mid-September 1897, as she completed the first draft of *Women and Economics,* she was hunting for a copy of *Dynamic Sociology* because, she explained to Gilman, "I am quite anxious to know if I should read it before publishing my book."[68] In early December, he presented her with a copy as a gift.[69] In October 1903, Charlotte Perkins Gilman referred to Ward's *Pure Sociology* (1903) in public lecture as "a remarkable book recently published" which compiled "an immense amount of indisputable fact" to prove the female "is the original and permanent thing in creation" and the male "is subsidiary." In the same lecture she also adopted Ward's nomenclature of andro- and gynaeco-centrism.[70] She peppered *Human Work* with allusions to Ward (cf. *HW*, 5, 164) and presented him with a copy of the book. He immediately thanked her "for the good words" and, a month later, replied more fully: "Well, I couldn't wait, so I have read your book. I could hear my own voice all the time. But, of course, it was not an echo. It is pitched much higher than I can strike and differs also entirely in *timbre.*"[71] Ward added in an essay published in 1906 that Gilman was the only contemporary reformer who approached social questions from a "cosmological perspective."[72] In the *Forerunner* in 1910, even as *The Man-Made World* was appearing serially, Gilman editorially urged "every woman who knows how to read" to find a copy of *Pure Sociology* and read at least the fourteenth chapter on "the phylogenetic forces" wherein Ward proposed a theory "new, original, wildly startling, intensely significant, and, in the world of ideas, revolutionary in the highest degree."[73] She reiterated the admonition in a prefactory note to the hardcover edition of *The Man-Made World,* which she dedicated to Ward. After its publication, she once more sent her mentor a copy of her work. He was deeply touched by the gesture, which he soon acknowledged: "I want to thank you so much for The Man-Made World, and especially for the Dedication, which I esteem a great honor, albeit couched in too extravagant terms . . . . No one is doing as much as you to propagate the truth about the sexes, as I have tried to set it forth."[74] Gilman "sometimes varied the language slightly," Mary Hill concludes, "but essentially she left Ward's arguments intact."[75]

Reviewers generally shared Ward's enthusiasm for *The Man-Made World*. Indeed, several compared it favorably to *Women and Economics*.[76] As usual, opinion was divided on the question of style, with the *Literary Digest* on the one hand granting that Gilman "writes interestingly, and at times vigorously," and the *Independent* on the other complaining "there is a hardness and bareness of style due to the fact that [Gilman] is a wit and not a humorist."[77] Reviewers agreed, however, that the work was an enlightening treatment of a significant issue. "It is a book just loaded with dynamite," according to the *New York Times*, written with "an undercurrent of burning indignation."[78] "The undeniable truth of many of her arraignments" and the reforms she proposed, added the *American Library Association Booklist*, "make the book interesting and stimulating."[79] Even a reviewer intensely critical of the aggressive tone of the treatise, T. D. A. Cockerell in the *Dial*, concluded it was "worth reading and will deserve and have a place in the history of thought."[80] Later, the book was "widely translated in Europe" (*L*, 306–7) and inspired the sociologist Edward A. Ross to include a chapter about "Women in a Man-Made World" in his book *The Social Trend* (1922).

Gilman cast a bas-relief of the splendid new world she envisioned in an extraordinary fragment of fiction published in 1907. She discussed this work with dispatch in her autobiography: An "enthusiast, starting a new magazine, engaged me to write a serial novel for him, but was punished for his rashness by the prompt failure of his venture" (*L*, 303). She might have added, however, that four issues of the magazine, the *Times*, appeared before the suspension, that three of them contained installments of her story "A Woman's Utopia," and that a fourth installment was printed and exists in page proofs among her papers at Radcliffe College. In all, perhaps a third of the projected novel is extant, and these chapters provide a revealing glimpse through Gilman's eyes of a world remade by women.

Like her three later utopian romances, "A Woman's Utopia" is narrated from the point of view of a man slowly converted from masculism to feminism.[81] This narrator, Morgan G. Street, seems to have been broadly modeled upon G. Houghton Gilman. Much as Street possesses a flair for languages and studied law at Harvard, for example, Houghton Gilman studied classical languages at Columbia and law at Johns Hopkins. Much as Street falls in love with "a sort of cousin" named Hope Cartwright who is "boiling over with ideas" for humanitarian reform, Gilman fell in love with his cousin Charlotte Perkins Stetson. Street is also a conservative, dubious about the prospects for social change. He accompanies Cartwright to meetings of the "preposterous R. G. U. Club," an organization he derisively nicknames the "argue" club: "It was a sort of debating society," he explains, composed of members "with the humanitarian bee in their bonnets, mad with the notion of helping the world." Among them are a businessman who finances model tenements, a Christian Socialist minister, and several women, each of whom specializes in cooking, child-culture, art, dressmaking, or housekeeping.

The story builds from a simple premise. Cartwright declines Street's proposal of marriage because their "ideas were antagonistic." In a pique, Street strikes upon a peculiar strategy to test their respective principles. He agrees to leave twenty of his twenty-five million dollars to the R. G. U. Club "to play with" for twenty years. Cartwright accepts his proposition: "In May, 1927, you can come back," she tells him. "I'll show you a happier country—and what's more, I'll return the twenty millions." Street spends the next twenty years "in travel and research," all the while, like Rip Van Winkle or Philip Nolan, ignorant of conditions in his native land. He returns to New York, as scheduled, in May 1927. Upon docking, he writes, "The first thing I noticed was the entire absence of smoke."[82] He is also relieved to learn that the yellow journalists of the Hearst stripe are out of business.

Street soon discovers even more dramatic changes in the status of women. As explains one of his guides through the new America, women a generation earlier "were maintained in a primitive relation to man, a subordinate, dependent position; taking no part in our social growth. This kept them like a lower race among us, and preserved in them the vices and weaknesses of the lower races. . . . Our women are people, now, I can tell you—and splendid ones. Wait till you see what they are doing in our schools, in city government, in business." During the years Street was away, women not only received the vote but began to exercise a salutary influence on "civic management."

These changes are best articulated and illustrated by Hope Cartwright. The narrator visits his cousin in her "charming apartment, high up" in a building on Riverside Drive, "with the wide Hudson spread before her, and the range of sunlit-glory from southeast to northwest." Gilman depicted the scene from experience, for she lived at the time in a similar apartment on Riverside Drive, on the top floor of the building, with a view of the Hudson and the sunset (*L,* 295–96). Cartwright recounts to her old antagonist how a "spiritual and practical" revival preached by the Christian Socialist in the R. G. U. Club had attracted and organized the "great mass of uneasy women" twenty years before. They had formed a political party to campaign for reform and, with Street's twenty millions, funded model projects in child-culture, apartment hotels, socialized industries, and municipal utilities. "In twenty years of aroused motherhood we have 'cleaned house' for our children; cleaned the streets, cleaned the water, cleaned the air," Cartwright declares. Moreover, women in 1927 enjoy economic independence, with 60 percent of them "at work now." Unfortunately, the contours of this utopia also conform to the nativist biases of its creator. Gilman paradoxically excused both exploitation of immigrant labor and imposition of immigration quotas. The story breaks off as Street visits the kitchenless home of a woman and mother who is both economically independent and happily married. He has revised his estimate of women and the potential for reform and, had the tale continued, he no doubt would have entered a "higher marriage" with Hope Cartwright.

For nearly a decade, Gilman had placed her work virtually at will in major American magazines and with major commercial publishers. Arthur Vance, editor of the *Pictorial Review,* credited her with "starting us off on the line to which we feel we owe our success, and that is trying to make a magazine for intelligent women to read."[83] However, as Gilman reflected in her memoirs, as the years passed "my work grew in importance but lost in market value," thus "I wrote more and sold less." Theodore Dreiser, who as editor of the *Delineator* accepted one of her essays on kitchenless homes, told her, "You should consider more what the editors want." But Gilman refused to compromise. She explained, "There are those who write as artists, real ones; they often find it difficult to consider what the editor wants" (*L,* 303–4). Or, as she had written earlier, "The artist catering to an employer does not grow, but deteriorates" (*HW,* 352). Her opinions were so controversial, she concluded, "it is a wonder that so many editors took so much of my work for so long." As "more and more of my stuff was declined" and "the manuscripts accumulated far faster than I could sell them," she tried a new tack (*L,* 304). If she could not write what editors and publishers wanted, she would become her own editor and publisher and write what she pleased. In late 1909, she launched her remarkable monthly magazine the *Forerunner*.

Chapter Four
The *Forerunner* Years

Charlotte Perkins Gilman single-handedly wrote, edited, and published a total of eighty-six issues of the *Forerunner* over seven years and two months. Each twenty-eight-page issue contained an installment of a novel and another serial work, usually nonfiction; a short story and a short essay on subjects which ranged from white slavery to noise pollution; and editorials, sermons, poems, book reviews, and commentary on current events. Each annual volume, by Gilman's own estimate, equaled four books of thirty-six thousand words and cost three thousand dollars to publish. The income from all sales and subscriptions, at a dime per issue and a dollar per year, totaled only half that amount. Moreover, Gilman began the magazine "with no capital except a mental one."[1] She raised the balance "by doing extra work in writing—outside of the 'four book' demands of the magazine, and as usual, lecturing" (*L*, 304–5). As she wrote Mabel Hay Mussey in March 1909, "Every cent I can rake and scrape is going into the New Baby!"[2] In 1911, Gilman toured the country for ten weeks, for example, and in June and July of 1913 she lectured in England, Germany, and Scandinavia while en route to and from the International Woman Suffrage Congress in Budapest. During the winter and spring of 1914, she delivered two memorable series of lectures in New York on "The Larger Feminism" and "Our Male Civilization" which attracted audiences as large as two hundred.[3] For a time, Gilman also employed "a good advertising man" to sell classified space in her magazine, but he resigned after explaining that he "could sell a page of *Scribner's Magazine* for several hundreds" more easily than a page in the *Forerunner* for twenty-five dollars (*L*, 306). She also refused to advertise products she could not personally endorse, a policy which "did not make for business success." She often expressed the hope that her "hungry child" would eventually become self-supporting, but it remained a dependent throughout its brief life.[4]

Still, as Gilman later wrote W. D. Howells, she was "well pleased" by the undertaking.[5] She understood from the first that the market appeal of the magazine was necessarily limited by the heterodoxies to which it was dedicated: a "practical, impersonal Deism," with "no concern for immortality or salvation"; utilitarianism; socialism and pacifism; the political and economic independence of women; and professionalized food-preparation and child-culture. The *Forerunner* was arguably more radical, certainly more ambitious in design, than the socialist *Progressive Woman*. She devoted the magazine, in her own words, to "the Near Sure Perfectly Possible Improvement of Life," and she advertised it was "only a suffrage paper because of its interest in women, and only a woman's paper because of its interest in humanity."[6] Some potential readers may have shared Gilman's perspective "on one point and some on two, but when it came to five or more distinct heresies" few were constrained to purchase the magazine (*L, 309–10). Though the subscription list was short, at least the *Forerunner* was widely circulated. Of the approximately fifteen hundred subscribers, nearly a hundred resided in Europe and Great Britain, with other readers scattered "as far afield as India and Australia."[7] The journal was also distributed by the Rand School of Science, where Gilman occasionally lectured; the National American Woman Suffrage Association; the Women's Political Union; and the Socialist Literature Company.[8]

Unfortunately, few critics, not even Howells—though Gilman twice sent him bound volumes—deigned to notice the magazine. Among the exceptions were reviewers for the *Chicago Evening Post* ("clear, sane, and entertaining"), the *Chicago Dial* ("a forceful and stimulating writer, with plenty of convictions and no lack of courage for them"), and the more exotic *Vegetarian Magazine* ("it is hoped that Charlotte Gilman is a vegetarian, thus making her more perfect").[9] Floyd Dell called the *Forerunner* "a remarkable journal" and Zona Gale declared its publication over seven years Gilman's "greatest single achievement."[10] Both Eugene V. Debs and Upton Sinclair publicly quoted from the magazine Gilman's poem "Child Labor."[11] On the other hand, Mary Austin carped that "Everything she wrote was in the same key." Austin eventually canceled her subscription to the "magazine with its terrible sameness, its narrow scope."[12] In all, Gilman issued in barely seven years the equivalent of twenty-eight books, including "Our Brains and What Ails Them," "Humanness," "Social Ethics," *What Diantha Did,* and *The Man-Made World*; three more utopian romances; dozens of short stories; four other novels "by which I definitely proved that I am not a novelist" (*L, 306); two other social treatises; and enough verse to fill an entire volume.

Reform Naturalism

According to standard literary histories, the fictional strategy of
naturalism collapsed at mid-century around an inherent contradiction. The literary naturalist ostensibly invented characters and set-
tings, observed behavior, and, like a scientist in a laboratory after
watching rats in a maze, recorded the operation of inexorable natural
laws. At least in theory, the naturalistic novel was a kind of lab report. In practice, however, novelists such as Zola, Dreiser, and Jack
London were never quite so detached, never quite so neutral or value-
free. As Malcolm Cowley has explained, "In writing their novels,
most of the naturalists pictured themselves as expressing a judgment
of life that was scientific, dispassionate, and, to borrow one of their
phrases, completely unmoral; but a better word for their attitude
would be 'rebellious.' Try as they would, they could not remain
merely observers. They had to revolt against the moral standards of
their time."[13] Literary naturalism was in theory positivistic and non-
teleological, in practice a yawp of protest and hope. Charles Walcutt
has concluded that "all 'naturalistic' novels exist in a tension between
determinism and its antithesis. The reader is aware of the opposition
between what the artist says about man's fate and what his saying it
affirms about man's hope."[14] Exhausted on the treadmill of this par-
adox, literary naturalism gasped its last in the mid-century war novels of Norman Mailer and James Jones.

The dogma of determinism was especially pronounced in American
naturalism because of the vogue the English philosopher Herbert
Spencer enjoyed in this country.[15] Whereas Darwin studied biological
organisms for evidence to buttress his theories of natural selection,
Spencer applied Darwin's theories to a model of social organizations
that paraded under the banner of social Darwinism. According to
Spencer, just as the fittest of each species in nature struggle for existence by adapting to hostile environment, the fittest human competitors best adapt to social conditions and accumulate wealth. The
natural laws that discriminate between biological types had governed
beneficently and unremittingly for millennia, Spencer claimed, and so
long as these laws operate without legislative interference they will
guarantee progress and prosperity for the nation and race. Arguing
from analogy to the biological world, Spencer offered a rationale for
economic laissez-faire that found ready ears among many American
industrialists (e.g., John D. Rockefeller and Andrew Carnegie), social

scientists (e.g., William Graham Sumner), and novelists (e.g., Dreiser and Jack London).

To reiterate: literary naturalists, in varying degrees, accepted the deterministic implications of this conservative social philosophy. Though Dreiser, for example, professed a brand of socialism, he admitted that his early reading of Spencer's *First Principles* "quite blew me, intellectually, to bits."[16] Though London too was a professed socialist, his autobiographical hero Martin Eden discovers principles in Spencer which organize "all knowledge for him, reducing everything to unity, elaborating ultimate realities."[17] Not coincidentally, the divided stream of American naturalism is most apparent in Dreiser's and London's works. In *The Financer* (1910), Dreiser grudgingly admired a ruthless predator-protagonist who, upon observing a lobster devour a squid, concludes that "men live on other men." In *The Sea Wolf* (1904), London portrayed with evident respect the *Übermensch* Wolf Larsen, who captains his ship by brute force and superior intellect. These novels evince no real faith in the efficacy of social reform, for Dreiser and London accepted the notion that the "struggle for existence" is the law of nature by which the unfit are eliminated.

In her fiction no less than in her essays and poetry, Charlotte Perkins Gilman rejected the doctrine of determinism embraced by canonical literary naturalists. In the very first issue of the *Forerunner*, for example, she referred to the "extreme loathsomeness" of London's stories.[18] Whereas the fiction of Dreiser, London, and others implicitly betrays a debt to social Darwinists like Spencer, Gilman erected her fictional world upon a reform Darwinian foundation laid by Lester Ward. However weak her inventions of plot and character, her didactic purpose led Gilman to adopt a fortunate literary strategy, a type of reform naturalism, which enabled her to transcend the contradiction of design and purpose inherent in conventional naturalism. In particular, Gilman wrote three utopian romances serialized in the *Forerunner* according to this strategy. These novels, all narrated by early twentieth-century American men, both satirize androcentric culture and describe the more humane world she expected to evolve from it.

Gilman set the first of these romances, *Moving the Mountain* (1911), in 1940, barely thirty years in the future. The narrator, John Robertson, whose name connotes masculine exclusivity, slips into a Tibetan crevice and a amnesiac void in 1910. He emerges to discover what Gilman, in the preface to the book, called "a baby Utopia, a little one that can grow." He learns to his dismay that in 1920 the American people opted for socialism, not a "return to normalcy," and over the next twenty years pushed past socialism to a New Religion. Robertson wonders whether "that old dream of Bellamy's" is merely "stalking abroad" until his sister, Ellen, the president of a co-educational college, explains to him that

we have no longer the fear of death—much less of damnation, and no such thing as "sin"; that the only kind of prison left is called a quarantine—that punishment is unknown but preventive means are of a drastic and sweeping nature such as we never dared think of before—that there is no such thing in the civilized world as poverty— no labor problem—no color problem—no sex problem—almost no disease—very little accident—practically no fires— that the world is rapidly being reforested—the soil improved; the output growing in quantity and quality; that no one needs to work over two hours a day and most people work four—that we have no graft—no adulteration of goods—no malpractice—no crime.

Women participate fully in the socialized economy of 1940, and the home is no longer a prison for either wife or child.

Like most utopian romances, *Moving the Mountain* contains more dialogue than plot. Robertson's brother-in-law and guide through the new world, Owen Montrose, spouts aphorisms from Lester Ward and tries to explain how "the amazing uprush of these thirty years was really due to the wholesale acceptance and application of the idea of evolution." Evidently a conservative Darwinist, Robertson is confused. "Evolution is the slowest of slow processes," he complains. "It took us thousands of dragging years to evolve the civilization of 1910, and you show me a 1940 that seems thousands of years beyond that." "Yes," Owen replies,

but what you call "evolution" was that of unaided nature. Social evolution is a distinct process. Below us, you see, all improvements had to be built into the stock—transmitted by heredity. The social organism is open to lateral transmission—what we used to call education. We never understood it. We thought it was to supply certain piles of information, mostly useless; or to develop certain qualities. . . . We know now that *the* social process is to constantly improve and develop society. This has a necessary corollary of improvement in individuals; but the thing that matters most is growth in the social spirit—and body.

A similar conversation occurs in the penultimate chapter of the romance between Robertson and a professor of ethics, Frank Borderson, whose views and name echo those of Lester Frank Ward. Robertson again wonders aloud how, "with people as they were," the world might be remade in little more than a generation. The professor, who clearly expresses Gilman's own views, retorts that "You are wrong in your premises, John. Human nature is, and was, just as good as the rest of nature. Two things kept us back—wrong conditions, and wrong ideas; we have changed both." According to Gilman, men need not live on other men, as Dreiser and his financier believed. More to the point, apart from the contrivances she employed to set the story in the future, Gilman was no less scientific than Dreiser, just as Ward was no less scientific than Spencer. It was possible for a literary naturalist, structuring fiction according to the principles of reform Darwinism, to transcend the divided stream.

Unfortunately, Gilman's millennial vision was blurred by a willingness to sanction gross violations of individual rights to realize the mass ideal. Immigrants who apply for residency in the new America must pass through a program of "Compulsory Socialization" for, as one character explains, "We have a standard of citizenship now—an idea of what people ought to be and how to make them so." No woman is "allowed to care for her children without proof of capacity" as determined by a governmental agency, "the Department of Child Culture." Men who contract venereal disease must register with "the Department of Eugenics." The press is also government-controlled. Incredibly, moreover, severely handicapped people and "certain classes of criminal and perverts" are not merely sterilized, a measure repugnant in its own right, but occasionally *executed* by order of the state: "We killed many hopeless degenerates, insane, idiots, and real perverts," Frank Borderson declares, "after trying our best powers of cure." Gilman mercifully failed to diagram the machinery by which a decision is reached to "amputate" persons, like diseased limbs, from the body politic.[19] Her dream of America circa 1940 was a curious blend of the bucolic and despotic. She issued the romance in single-volume format early in 1912, at the height of the eugenics craze, and reviewers in such periodicals as the *Independent* and the *New York Times* ignored her implicit authoritarianism to remark in particular upon the ease with which the inert mountain had been moved.[20]

Gilman later serialized two more utopian romances in the *Forerunner* which dramatically contrast a woman-made and a man-made

world. Structurally, these romances also betray the influence of, respectively, Edward Bellamy's *Looking Backward* and W. D. Howells'
Altrurian romances. Like Bellamy, Gilman portrayed in *Herland*
(1915) a colorless native of the workaday world suddenly and unwit-
tingly translated to a heaven on earth. Like Howells in *A Traveler
from Altruria,* Gilman adopted the opposite premise, an innovation on
the utopian formula, in her sequel *With Her in Ourland* (1916). She
recognized this innovation in an early review of Howells's book: "We
are shown the novel spectacle of an inhabitant of Arcadian lands
transferred into the midst of our social confusion, suffering and un-
rest."[21] She reiterated the point in one of her early lectures: Howells
"gives us in his 'A Traveler from Altruria' not one view of heaven,
but heaven's puzzled view of earth!"[22]

Vandyke Jennings, the narrator of *Herland,* is a sociologist by
training and, as the story opens, a masculinist by inclination. With
two male companions, he stumbles upon a lost civilization, an undis-
covered country populated entirely by women who reproduce par-
thenogenetically. They decide to explore.

Presently there lay before us at the foot of a long hill the town or village
we were aiming for. We stopped and studied it.

Jeff drew a long breath. "I wouldn't have believed a collection of houses
could look so lovely," he said.

"They've got architects and landscape gardeners in plenty, that's sure,"
agreed Terry. . . . "Those big white ones are public buildings evidently. . . ."

The place had an odd look, more impressive as we approached. . . . It
certainly was different from any towns we had ever seen.

"There's no dirt," said Jeff suddenly. "There's no smoke," he added after
a little. . . . As we neared the center of the town the houses stood thicker,
ran together as it were, grew into rambling palaces grouped among parks
and open squares. . . .

Van and his friends soon turn a corner "into a broad paved space"
(*Hrld,* 18–19) where they are arrested by a cadre of Herlanders.

This scene is noteworthy for several reasons. Above all, Gilman in-
timated that the Herland commonwealth is superior to the man-made
world. She embroidered the story on the frame of Ward's ideas.
Moreover, the passage is strongly reminiscent of a similar scene in
Looking Backward. In Bellamy's story, Julian West, revived from his
long sleep, stands spellbound at the sight of twenty-first-century
Boston:

At my feet lay a great city. Miles of broad streets, shaded by trees and lined with fine buildings, for the most part not in continuous blocks but set in larger or smaller inclosures, stretched in every direction. Every quarter contained large open squares filled with trees, among which statues glistened and fountains flashed in the later afternoon sun. Public buildings of a colossal size and an architectural grandeur unparalleled in my day raised their stately piles on every side. Surely I had never seen this city nor one comparable to it before.

Much like Gilman's character, West was struck in particular by "the complete absence of chimneys and their smoke."[23] In addition to the stylistic parallel, both Gilman and Bellamy invented ideal worlds whose appeal was essentially nostalgic. Gilman modeled her gynaecocentric utopia upon the matriarchal family she knew as a child, and Bellamy modeled his smokeless Boston of 2000 A.D. upon the preindustrial village he remembered from his boyhood.

Gilman's aside that the capital of Herland resembles an "exposition" also suggests her familiarity with contemporary principles of urban planning. The most prominent American city planner of the era, Daniel Burnham (1846–1912), had designed, in the early 1890s, the Columbian Exposition, a baroque assemblage of parks, monumental buildings, and boulevards in imitation Renaissance style constructed a few miles from the Chicago Loop and popularly called "the White City." Gilman had often expressed a wish in her diary to attend the Exposition in person.[24] In December 1893, she praised Howells in the *Impress* for treating in his "Letters of an Altrurian Traveler," then under serialization in *Cosmopolitan,* the "impressions of that Utopian stranger at the World's Fair." As she noted, "To the Altrurian the White City is more natural, more life-like, than any of the black cities where we are content to work for the living that is never lived."[25] Burnham's plans for the White City subsequently inspired a movement known among architects as the City Beautiful, and Burnham later executed plans for malls and civic centers in the cities of Cleveland, Manila, San Francisco, and, most notably, Chicago. In each case, Burnham proposed to construct massive public buildings and monuments in a zone distinct from the residential districts of the city and to use space and monuments to sublime effect, as in the original Exposition. As Gilman wrote in 1903, "The White City by the lake was an inspiration to myriad lives, and wrought a lovely change in architecture" (*H,* 152). In 1915, elsewhere in the same issue of the *Forerunner* in which she described her ideal Herland city, she alluded to its model: "Since the World's Fair at Chicago in 1893, we have had our dream cities. Soon we can have them real."[26] Gilman's ideal metropolis, in short, seems to marry the conceptions of Ward, Bellamy, and Burnham.

At first, Van and his friends Terry and Jeff are blinded to the wonders of the Herland civilization. "We were not in the least 'advanced' on the woman question, any of us, then," he ruefully confesses. The "intensely masculine" Terry considered it from his androcentric perspective "a sort of sublimated summer resort" filled with women eager for his attention. He thought pretty women "just so much game and homely ones not worth considering." At the other extreme, the genteel sentimentalist Jeff "idealized women in the best Southern style" and "was always looking for a chance to 'protect' or 'serve' them" though they might need "neither protection nor service" (*Hrld*, 89). Van occupied a middle ground between the two "and used to argue learnedly about the physiological limitations of the sex" (*Hrld*, 7–9). "This is a *civilized* country," he at once declares, so "there must be men" (*Hrld*, 11).

Slowly Van revises his estimate of women and the woman-made world of Herland. Figuratively reborn, like Julian West, into an advanced civilization (*Hrld*, 24–25), he recounts the story of his conversion retrospectively. "It interested me profoundly to note and study the subtle difference between these women and other women, and try to account for them," he explains. "In the matter of personal appearance, there was a great difference. They all wore short hair, some few inches at most; some curly, some not; all light and clean and fresh-looking" (*Hrld*, 30). They also wear light and functional tunics which, unlike the usual fashion, do not accentuate sexual characteristics. The Herlanders are, after all, fully human beings, not oversexed, underdeveloped females. They were peace-loving, "had no kings, and no priests, and no aristocracies. They were sisters, and as they grew, they grew together—not by competition, but by united action" (*Hrld*, 60). Mary A. Hill justly describes the romance as "the most explicit statement of Gilman's admiration and love for women."[27]

At the outset, Van also articulates orthodox social Darwinian dogma. Asked to explain why poverty exists in his country, for example, he contends "that the laws of nature require a struggle for existence, and that in the struggle the fittest survive, and the unfit perish. In our economic struggle, I continued, there was always plenty of opportunity for the fittest to reach the top, which they did, in great numbers, particularly in our country" (*Hrld,* 63). He realizes with a start, however, that Herland is a cooperative community. At the extremes, Terry ignores the harmony of the state ("Women cannot cooperate—it's against nature") and Jeff, who compares Herland to "an enormous anthill," simply acknowledges it ("Women are the natural cooperators, not men"). Children, who are given neither gender-specific first names nor surnames, are reared communally, as in the modern Israeli kibbutz. Indeed, the "children in this country are [its] one center and focus" (*Hrld,* 66). The Herlanders practice a benign matriarchial religion and worship a goddess of mother-love. Even their games are noncompetitive, requiring skill and finesse rather than brute strength (*Hrld,* 32, 41). Van concludes that "these ultra-women, inheriting only from women, had eliminated not only certain masculine characteristics" but "so much of what we had always thought essentially feminine" (*Hrld,* 57). They have been free to realize their full human potential, not merely to develop their sexual traits, according to the terms of Ward's gynaecocentric theory. Unfortunately, like most utopian communities depicted in fiction, Herland is so benign and static it is as dull as "an old, established, perfectly-run country place" (*Hrld,* 99). Like angels in paradise, the Herlanders have no problems to occupy their time.

By the end of the novel, convinced of the natural superiority of women, Van has been converted to feminism and socialism. Like good reform Darwinists, the Herlanders, he learns, have met the challenges of population growth and limited resources not

by a "struggle for existence" which would result in an everlasting writhing mass of underbred people trying to get ahead of one another—some few on top, temporarily, many constantly crushing out underneath, a hopeless substratum of paupers and degenerates, and no serenity or peace for anyone, no possibility for really noble qualities among the people at large. . . . Not at all. They sat down at council together and thought it out. Very clear, strong thinkers they were. They said: "With our best endeavors this country will support about so many people, with the standard of peace, comfort, health, beauty, and progress we demand. Very well. That is all the people we will make." (*Hrld,* 68)

Much as the Herlanders selectively breed cats to control the mice and mole population and thus to protect their crops, they practice "negative eugenics" to control and maintain their own population.

With the fortuitous appearance of the male intruders, moreover, the nation may once again exploit the advantages of heterosexual reproduction. Ever the scientist armed with a theory, Van is unable to account for "so much divergence" among the three million Herlanders "without cross-fertilization." Though some of the so-called "Over Mothers" attribute it to superior education and mutation, Van convinces them that "there was more chance of improvement in greater physical variation" (*Hrld*, 77–78). As Gilman later explained in her own voice, parthenogenesis is not a desirable means of reproduction because "Fertilization is a higher process, a superior process."[28] As a nation, the Herlanders eagerly anticipate the next evolutionary step promised by dual parentage, variously dubbed "the Great Change," "the Great New Hope," and "the Great Adventure," in fact an elaborate experiment in stirpiculture.

By reversing the traditional roles in the mirror she held to the reader, Gilman treated courtship rituals with sardonic wit. The men become sex objects, competing among themselves for the attention of the females. While Terry, Jeff, and Van are plumed like peacocks whenever they appear in public, the women, like the peahen, actually exercise the prerogatives of sexual selection. "All that time we were in training they studied us, analyzed us, prepared reports about us," Van reports, "and this information was widely disseminated all about the land" (*Hrld*, 88). Each of the men is confounded to discover that he arouses no sexual passion in the Herlanders whom he meets. As Van explains, "There was no sex-feeling to appeal to, or practically none. Two thousand years' disuse had left very little of the instinct" (*Hrld*, 92). However, each of them at length is paired with a young Herlander who both befriends him and is willing to hazard the "experiment" (*Hrld*, 88–89). Whereas Jeff's reverent devotion puzzled his friend Celis and postponed their marriage and Terry and Alima "quarreled and parted, re-met and re-parted," Van and Ellador "grew to be close friends" (*Hrld*, 90). Still, Celis, Alima, and Ellador neither blush, nor flirt, nor grow jealous, nor coyly submit to embraces. As Terry complains, they have "none of that natural yielding which is woman's greatest charm" (*Hrld*, 98). Even Van concludes "these women were not provocative" and laments they had "not the faintest idea of that *solitude à deux* we are so fond of" (*Hrld*, 125, 128).

Nor are the marriages uniformly successful, given the expectations of the male partners. Terry tries to master Alima and exercise his "marital rights," only to be rebuffed, arrested, and expelled from the country. Jeff and Celis apparently engage in intercourse for purposes of procreation only. Ellador and Van are affectionate, but they hardly observe the "custom of marital indulgence." Van describes Ellador at the consummation of their marriage in imagery unmistakably aloof and cool: "She trembled in my arms, as I held her close, kissing her hungrily. But there rose in her eyes that look I knew so well, that remote clear look as if she had gone far away even though I held her beautiful body so close, and was now on some snowy mountain regarding me from a distance" (*Hrld,* 138). Rather than advancing from passion to friendship, as in most conventional marriages, their love is nurtured by mutual respect before it finds sexual expression. Van revealingly compares his love for Ellador as "coming home to mother" and welcomes the sense "of getting home; of being clean and rested; of safety and yet freedom; of love that was always there, warm like sunshine in May, not hot like a stove or a featherbed" (*Hrld,* 142). Still, they choose to accompany Terry into exile, ostensibly because Ellador is keen to visit "the Rest of the World," actually because the author wished to depict its terrors through her eyes. The tale was so remarkable that it was reprinted in a modern edition in 1979 and immediately hailed as a "lost feminist utopian novel," though it was hardly lost in the same sense as Gilman's "A Fallen Sister" or "A Woman's Utopia."

In the sequel, *With Her in Ourland* (1916), Van and Ellador travel abroad in a world at the brink of war. Though a limp vehicle for satire, Gilman's debt to Ward is no less apparent than in her earlier utopian fictions. Van realizes in the course of this story that "there is no getting around Lester Ward. . . . No one can study biology and sociology much and not see that on the first physiological lines the female is the whole show, so to speak, or at least most of it." By exposing the humane Ellador to the inhumanity of the masculinist world at war, Gilman underscored the vulgarity and cruelty of that world. Like Howells's Altrurian, the Herlander recoils in dismay from the savage state in which the readers live. Moreover, much as the Altrurian visits the 1893 Columbian Exposition in Chicago, the Herlander tours the 1915 World's Exposition in San Francisco, an episode Gilman modeled in part upon her own visit to the Exposition.[29] "You are like an Investigating Committee from another world," Van declares Ellador is especially incensed by cultural and military imperialism and, like "an eminent surgeon engaged in a first-class operation," she diagnoses the pathological social condition.

After several months amid the "dim dirtiness," the "brutal noise and the unsatisfied, unsatisfying people going so hurriedly about after their food," Van and Ellador withdraw to the sanctuary of Herland.[30] The romance ends on an ironic note, as Gilman inverts the story of Christ's nativity. Though capable of virgin birth, Ellador conceives sexually the promise of a new age, and bears the first son born to a mated Herlander in two thousand years.

The decline of naturalism, both Walcutt and Philip Rahv agree, can be traced to the naturalists' failure to marry form and content.[31] Walcutt even protests that the phrase "naturalistic style" is oxymoronic. Insofar as the fiction was faithful to the positivistic premises of naturalism, he contends, it precluded stylization, and vice-versa. Better than any writer Walcutt and Rahv mention, however, Charlotte Perkins Gilman resolved the contradiction. Her philosophical orientation, her reform naturalism, was expressed better in utopian than in realistic fiction.

Other Fiction

With rare exceptions, the stories Gilman published during the *Forerunner* years were fantasies with a feminist message, as in the case of her utopian fiction, or illustrations of women's economic independence. The stories in the former category tend to be whimsical and parabolic, stories in the latter contrived and repetitive. In "If I Were a Man" (1914), for example, one morning "pretty little Mollie Mathewson" is transformed into her husband Gerald. S/he enjoys such novel experiences as the sensation of money in pockets and, at the office, s/he defends women from the aspersions cast by men (*CPGR,* 32–38). Similarly, in "When I Was a Witch" (1910), the narrator on Halloween suddenly acquires the magical power to realize her wishes. Over the course of several days, she metes out punishment to fit the offense to those who abuse animals, sell bad milk or meat, or short-change customers. "Then I wished similar things for all manner of corporations and officials," she adds, whereupon "there was a sudden conscientious revival all over the country." At her desire, newspapers begin to print their lies, slander, and ignorant mistakes in different shades of ink. Thus the narrator silently reforms the world much as Charlotte Perkins Gilman reinvented it in her imagination. Unfortunately, when the narrator wishes that women "might realize Womanhood at last" nothing happens for "this magic which had fallen on me was black magic—and I had wished white." Worse yet, her vain wish "stopped all the other things that were working so nicely" (*CPGR,* 21–31). In all, the story seems to betray the author's usually unspoken fear that she might fail as a reformer, that concrete institutions after all might withstand the changes she imagined would occur. In a third fantasy, "Dr. Clair's Place" (1915), Gilman proposed an ideal resolution to her predicament as a young wife thirty years before. She outlined in this tale how a female physician might treat neurasthenia. Unlike male counterparts such as Weir Mitchell, whose prognoses presumed the fragility of the "weaker sex," Willy Clair prescribes for her patients a regimen of work and amusement. "The trouble with Sanatoriums," she explains, "is that the sick folks have nothing to do but sit about and think of themselves and their 'cases.' " Instead, her patients read, weave, garden, swim, even climb mountains—and recover their strength and vitality.[32] The story was inspired, at least in part, by Gilman's visits early in the century to Dr. Mary Jacobi, who prescribed various stimulants, including low-grade electrical shock, to increase her patients' energy level.[33]

Gilman's parables of economic independence were more heavy-handed, formulaic, and predictable than her feminist fantasies. In each case, the protagonist becomes independent when she is separated, at least temporarily, from her husband and she resolves to improve the occasion, often with the aid of another woman who acts as her patron. In "The Widow's Might" (1911), for example, a middle-aged woman who nursed her late husband through his last illness and to whom he deeded his property declares to her grown children her intention to enjoy her remaining years. "Thirty years I've given you—and your father," she observes, matter-of-factly. "Now I'll have thirty years of my own." To their surprise and dismay, she plans to travel throughout the world and live on the income from the family ranch (*CPGR,* 98–106). Similarly, in "Mrs. Beazley's Deeds" (1911), the protagonist is counseled by "the best woman lawyer in New York" to "make a stand" against her ne'er-do-well husband for the sake of her children and refuse to deed her inherited property over to him. Mrs. Beazley eventually opens a boardinghouse and becomes economically self-reliant while her husband is compelled to flee the state to escape his creditors.[34] The title-character in "An Honest Woman" (1911) settles an old score with the man who abandoned her and their infant daughter. Over the years she "has won Comfort, Security, and Peace" as a respectable hosteler, and she is free to spurn the advances of her gold-digging ex-lover when he reappears (*CPGR*, 75–86).

Gilman occasionally illustrated in these tales her notion that the economic independence of women would improve and refine the marital institution. In "Mrs. Elder's Idea" (1912) for example, a middle-aged woman refuses to follow her husband into retirement in the country, takes an apartment near their old home in the city, and begins a career as a "professional shopper" or buyer. Though angry at first, her husband soon "found that two half homes and half a happy wife were really more satisfying than one whole home, and a whole unhappy wife, withering in discomfort."[35] In "Their Home" (1912), a woman manages the family business so successfully that she enables her husband to join a scientific expedition. Upon his return, each of them enjoys a career and the freedom to love the other more fully.[36]

Unfortunately, the four other novels Gilman serialized in the *Forerunner* suffered all of the liabilities of her didactic fiction without the grace of brevity. Moreover, she hardly embraced in these potboilers the literary program she announced in *The Man-Made World* or such later essays as "Coming Changes in Literature." With the changing status of women, Gilman thought authors would discover new fields for fiction, such as "the growing girl, looking forward to her mother-power with highest ambition, tenderest hope, profoundest joy."[37] Yet she ignored such subjects in her four late, ostensibly realistic novels of manners. Each of these tales is fundamentally a conventional, sentimental romance with faint feminist overtones.

In *The Crux* (1911), Gilman complicated the romance by portraying one of the lovers as a syphilitic. The young New England heroine, Vivian Lane, falls in love with Morton Elder, a scrapegrace who possesses "the rough good looks and fluent manner which easily find their way to the good will of many female hearts." One of Vivian's friends, Mrs. Adela St. Cloud, recommends she adopt a traditional woman's role, "to face a life of utter renunciation" and marry Morton in order to reform him. A more pragmatic friend, the physician Jane Bellair, preaches *carpe diem*. "Break away now, my dear, and come West," she urges. "You can get work—start a kindergarten or something." Like Molly Stark Wood in Owen Wister's *The Virginian*, one of Gilman's favorite novels,[38] Vivian has inherited "a store of quiet strength from some Pilgrim Father or Mother" and resolves to strike out for the West. Incredibly, all of the major characters eventually converge in Colorado. There St. Cloud again urges Vivian to "make a new man" of Morton, to undertake his reformation through love and marriage. Bellair urges her to break with him, for she has learned he has contracted venereal disease during a period of dissipation and debauchery. "I love him," Vivian protests, echoing hundreds of romantic heroines. "Will you tell that to your crippled children?" Bellair responds. "Will they understand it if they are idiots?" Obviously, "this is no case for idealism and exalted emotion." Vivian accedes to reason, breaks her engagement with Morton, and eventually marries a mature man who had been disappointed in love when young.[39] Despite its predictable resolution and denouement, Gilman issued the story in single-volume format early in 1912, and the *Independent* noted in its review that she pricked the "bubble of perverse tradition. . . harshly but with exemplary thoro[ugh]ness."[40].

Gilman serialized two utterly banal stories over the next two years. In *Mag-Marjorie* (1912), the protagonist, as a sixteen-year-old ugly duckling, is seduced and impregnated by a villainous young physician who abandons her. Mag is taken under wing by the philanthropic Mary Yale, who helps her fabricate her own drowning à la Huck Finn, carries her to Europe to school, and places her infant daughter in a foster home until she is able to care for her. "I'll give you my name," Miss Yale promises. "I'll take care of you—and yours! You shall start clear in another country—and make good!" A decade later, Margaret Yale, as she is now known, has become an eminent surgeon and a beautiful woman. Upon her return to the States, she immediately crosses paths with Richard Armstrong, the father of her child, who fails to recognize her. He falls in love with her and presses his suit, only to meet with the deserved rebuff. Meanwhile, Armstrong's friend and fellow physician Henry Newcomb has recognized Mag and also fallen in love with her, but keeps his own counsel. After he sees the distraught Armstrong hurry from her home, he proposes to her both a merger of medical practices and marriage. As he explains, with an unconsciously patronizing air, "You are to me like a beautiful widow—if I think of that at all. And as to the main fact—which is Dolly—why I love the child." Margaret Yale accepts both of his proposals and receives from him a new name—Marjorie—as if to signal her newfound respectability.[41]

The plot of the equally insipid *Won Over* (1913) turns on a slight misunderstanding. The tale centers on the plight of Stella Widfield, a conventional, middle-class wife who, after her children are grown, lives entirely for her husband Morgan, to his consternation. "It would

be a lot easier if you did care for something on earth besides me—
had other interests in life," he tells her. She meets a radical play-
wright and other literary figures, tries her hand at writing for magazines, and soon acquires a modest reputation among editors. To be
sure, "The little things that Stella did were not masterpieces, but
they were distinctive, original, new, and caught the popular taste
more suddenly than many a greater thing." Unfortunately, Morgan
is as nonplussed by her success as he had been bored by her languor,
especially when he overhears her rehearsing a scene with the play-
wright and fails to understand she was only reading lines. When he
realizes his mistake, they are soon reconciled; indeed, the conclusion
seems forced and contrived, his earlier objections to his wife's em-
ployment too quickly forgotten in the final paragraphs.[42]

Like most of her fiction, Gilman's final novel, *Benigna Machiavelli*
(1914), is an idealized roman à clef. The preternaturally wise narrator
is, as her name suggests, a benign Machiavelli. As she asserts, "I was
an infant prodigy in common sense, that's all; just plain intelligence,
with, of course, that splendid Machiavellian streak thrown in." She
has a loving sister whom she protects from a designing rogue; a
mother whom she sets up in business; an impractical father whom she
dispatches to relatives in Scotland; and a suitor whom she admires.
At twenty-one, the age at which the author had acceded to an entan-
gling alliance with Walter Stetson, her idealized persona Benigna
Machiavelli has set her own house in order and is ready to devote her
life to projects of social reformation.[43]

In all, Charlotte Perkins Gilman admitted in her autobiography
that her fiction, "especially the novels, which are poor," required especial care in "composition and were more difficult" to write than her
nonfiction. Fortunately, however pronounced her loss of creative
power, her early bout with neurasthenia had not robbed her of "the
power of expression" or "the faculty of inner perception, of seeing the
relation of facts and their consequence" (*L,* 100). She exploited these
skills in many of the miscellaneous essays and reviews she wrote for
the *Forerunner.*

Critical Miscellany

Gilman filled many of the pages of the *Forerunner,* especially in the
later years, with topical comment on art, politics, and current events.
She heartily approved the dancing of Isadora Duncan, for example,

though she was disgusted by the Armory Exhibition of 1913 and the advent of modernism in the plastic arts.[44] Whereas her first four nonfiction serials were well-organized treatises on androcentrism and social economics, moreover, Gilman's final two serials were disjointed essays on the absurdities of contemporary fashion and the increasing threat of world war. In *The Dress of Women* (1915), she merely updated her old proposals for dress reform, often echoing as well the chapter in Veblen's *The Theory of the Leisure Class* on "Dress as an Expression of the Pecuniary Culture."[45] The twelve installments of *Growth and Combat* (1916) were little more than a quiltwork compendium of tiresome editorials on such topics as cut-throat competition, the sinking of the *Lusitania,* and the German national character. In addition, Gilman often exploited the opportunity to defend or reward her acquaintances publicly in the pages of the magazine. She praised without stint books by her old friends from California, John Barry and Harriet Howe, as well as novels by her new friend Zona Gale,[46] Gilman conducted a salon of sorts at her home on Riverside Drive frequented by, among others, Emma Goldman and Mary Austin, and she in turn favorably reviewed Goldman's *Anarchism and Other Essays* (1910) and Austin's *A Woman of Genius* (1912).[47] She also favorably noticed *Sylvia's Marriage* (1914), a new novel by her occasional correspondent Upton Sinclair.[48]

Despite the potpourri of topical comment with which she filled each issue, Gilman did not attempt to appeal to broad or eclectic tastes. Through the years she emphasized several specific issues in the pages of the *Forerunner.* She endorsed the right of women "to refuse to bear" more children than they chose and to receive instruction in methods of contraception, even as she lamented the sex-mania of young people and excoriated Freud and the psychoanalysis cult. She shared with other feminists of her generation rigidly conventional views on sexual matters, often reiterating her conviction that "the normal purpose of sex-union is reproduction" and that "its continuous repetition, wholly disassociated with this use, results in a disproportionate development of the primary sex emotions and functional capacities."[49] She equated erotic love with base selfishness, as in a poem published in the magazine:[50]

> There are six mighty loves, not counting Eros.
> Love of the things that please us, mere attraction;
> Love after good received, reactive, grateful;

Love born of likeness, leading on to friendship;
Love built of admiration, worship's roadway;
Love based on usage, as for home and country;
And love that gives and serves, the love of mothers.

Eros may fail in all, and love stand loveless;
Attracted downward, to things base, unpleasing;
Repudiating benefit, ungrateful;
Drawn to unlikeness, into nameless discord;
Despising oftentimes the thing it chooses;
Finding in usage weariness and hatred;
All taking, nothing giving, wholly selfish.

European feminists such as Ellen Key, she averred, may aspire to personal or sexual liberation, but American feminists generally prefer to devote their lives to social service and the general welfare.[51] To her dismay, however, after the World War, after the approval of woman suffrage, younger American women adopted a different agenda. William O'Neill concludes that "their sexual views more than anything else" distinguished "the older feminists" of this era from a younger generation of American women "moved by quite different ambitions," and this "blind spot was true even of a woman like Charlotte Perkins Gilman."[52]

She continued over the years to demand the vote for women, though she focused not on the immediate goal of amending the Constitution but on the long-term effects of mobilizing the new voters. In 1911, she collected and privately published in a pamphlet entitled *Suffrage Songs and Verses* twenty-five of her poems on feminist themes, including "She Walketh Veiled and Sleeping," "Mother to Child," and "Wedded Bliss." She also frequently discussed over the years the wisdom of a political party composed exclusively of women. She was of two minds on the issue, refining or changing her position as the political winds shifted. Before 1912, she promoted the idea of a Woman's party. During the campaign of 1912, however, like her friend Jane Addams she endorsed the Progressive party of Theodore Roosevelt and added, early in 1913, that "We need, not a 'Woman's Party,' but certainly a Woman's Platform."[53] By 1916, she had again shifted her stand, proposing a caucus or league of women voters to accelerate the campaign for suffrage even while tendering a tepid endorsement of Woodrow Wilson's bid for reelection.[54]

No other single issue aroused her indignation during this period as did a local school board policy to dismiss women teachers who married. Male teachers who married, of course, were not liable to penalty. "Married women are not desired in our schools; not allowed; they are specifically discriminated against," Gilman justly complained.[55] The policy cut squarely against the grain of her hopes for economically emancipated womanhood, for women who both enjoy a happy marriage and prosper in a career. In particular, Gilman rallied to the defense of Clara Chess and Henrietta Rodman, the former a married teacher "who applied for a year's leave of absence, which was refused; sent in her resignation, which was not accepted; and was then discharged for 'neglect of duty' by a vote of twenty-four to nothing," the latter "a teacher of long experience and unquestioned efficiency" who "offended the prejudices of the dominant majority in the Board; first, by having ideas of which they disapproved; second, by expressing them; third, by marrying, and fourth, by presuming to keep her own name."[56] "Henrietta was a school teacher who lived on the lunatic fringe," Mary Austin observed, less charitably. She "got herself in wrong with the school board and was suspended for a year, but she won out in the end."[57] On her part, Gilman roundly condemned the "archaic position" on such questions adopted by the New York "educational dictators," especially one member of the board, Abraham Stern, who stoutly declared on the public record that "It is impossible to be a good mother and a good teacher."[58] She was predictably incensed by the remark, and she burlesqued the attitude unmercifully in a brief poem, excerpted as follows:[59]

> Abraham Stern, of the New York Schools,
> Is not to be classed among knaves or fools,
> But stands with the Wise, the Strong, the Good,
> In defense of Sacred Motherhood.
> . . . .
> As far as Abraham's arm can reach
> Mothers shall not be allowed to teach,
> Nor teachers to wed—as others should—
> Oh Grand Defender of Motherhood!

Partly as a result of the public outcry, Stern eventually was forced to resign from the school board and the discriminatory policy was abandoned.

Gilman also recurrently addressed issues of peace and war in the *Forerunner*. "I am a pacifist, of settled conviction," she wrote. Brushfire wars throughout the world proved, in her opinion, "the immediate practical necessity for the beginnings of world-federation."[60]

Like Charles and Mary Beard, whose economic interpretations of history she occasionally cited,[61] Gilman believed the profit motive perhaps caused, certainly exacerbated international conflict. By the same token, she heralded socialism as the harbinger of peace: "By millions and millions the working men of the world are realizing that whoever may profit by [war], they do not."[62] She viewed the Balkan war with horror and strenuously opposed the adventurism of the expeditionary force detailed to Mexico in 1914.[63] As war in Europe widened, she abhorred the senseless death and destruction while advancing the hope "born of the very magnitude of the evil" that the conflict might hasten the political unification of the continent, the inauguration of universal peace, and the full participation of women in reconstructed European society.[64] She anticipated the eventual evolution of a world government and even published in the *Forerunner* an anthem of allegiance for it, "Song for the World's Flag."[65] In 1920, after the armistice, she became an outspoken advocate of the League of Nations.[66]

As the war continued and the United States tilted its policy of strict neutrality toward the Allies, Gilman sailed with the tide. In the last two volumes of the magazine, she often vented in strident cadences her disaffection with the German nation. She favorably reviewed Owen Wister's rabidly anti-German diatribe *The Pentacost of Calamity* (1915), for example, and she attacked H. L. Mencken for, among his myriad sins, championing Theodore Dreiser, another writer with a German surname and sympathies. "Mr. Men[c]ken certainly does not belong in this country," she stated matter-of-factly.[67] While "perhaps the most socially developed of any civilized state," Gilman wrote in mid-1916, Germany had evolved "so imperfectly, so unevenly, as to become a very Frankenstein among the nations." She argued that the German national character was flawed by a streak of imperialism: "The peculiar responsibility of Germany in our present plague of war lies in the mental power of the people and their misuse of it." Indeed, "If Germany had Australia and no ships, she might become perfect without hurting anybody. Perhaps another planet would be better, nearer the sun—or Mars."[68] "When the war came, in 1914," Zona Gale later reflected, "after having preached all her life the unity of man and the need for human growth, she sided unconditionally with the allies and spoke of the German nation as criminally insane. This was a surprise to most of those who knew her, an utter contradiction of thought."[69] The shift was so pronounced, so unexpected, it probably alienated some of Gilman's readers and doomed her efforts to sustain the magazine. Margaret Sanger, the leading American advocate of birth control, censured Gilman at the time for becoming "a reactionary who lost courage by obtaining too much publicity."[70] Mary Austin later complained that she "had become a Socialist of the narrowest mold" and added that "After a time I lost touch with her; so did her other friends."[71] Gilman had finally become an anachronism.

Early in 1916, she decided to discontinue publication of the magazine at the end of the year. She had "relieved the pressure of what I had to say," as she explained the decision to her readers. Moreover, she could not longer afford to subsidize its printing costs. She had concluded, regretfully, that "there are not enough people who want the magazine to support it; and it is sociologically incorrect to maintain an insufficiently desired publication."[72] She advertised her continued availability for lectures and she published plans to issue eventually in separate volumes many of the best stories, essays, and poems written for the magazine.[73] "I could not have accomplished so much work in the same time any other way!" she wrote W.D. Howells.[74] Unfortunately, at the age of fifty-six, Charlotte Perkins Gilman virtually retired from the public eye. Four months after the final issue of her magazine appeared, the United States entered the Great War and dashed her hopes for a millennium of peace.

Chapter Five
Retirement and Denouement

"After seven years of the *Forerunner* I had no impulse to write for some time," Gilman observed in her autobiography. "I had said, fully and freely, the most important things I had to say" (*L,* 327). Briefly, between March and December 1919, the only period of her life that she drew a regular salary, she contributed a daily column to the *New York Tribune* syndicate. She gave her "short bits" such provocative titles as "Hats with Whiskers" and "If I Was a Horse" and touched on familiar ideas as well as on such topical subjects as the Russian revolution and the postwar housing shortage, but she failed "to reach and hold the popular taste." She also spent six weeks on a tour arranged by "one of the smaller Chautauquas" lecturing in "very small towns in rather backward regions mostly." Unfortunately, she added, "As a Chautauqua lecturer I was as much of a failure as in the pleasant platitudes of newspaper syndicates" (*L,* 310–11). Still, the tour underscored for Gilman the limitations of urban living. Most people who reside in cities, she complained in her syndicated column in August 1919, know little "of the beauty of the earth."[1] Indeed, one of the recurrent themes in her work, increasingly emphasized late in her career, was the problems and potential of the modern industrial city.

Urban Plans

During her literary apprenticeship in California, during her most productive period in New York, and especially after she suspended publication of the *Forerunner,* Gilman addressed questions of city design in her work. As she would write in one of the poems collected in *In This Our World* (1893),

> Woman's beauty fades and flies,
> In the passing of the years,
> With the falling of the tears,
> With the lines of toil and stress;

City's beauty never dies,—
Never while her people know
How to love and honor so
Her immortal loveliness.
(*ITOW*, 90)

Fortunately, her utopian enthusiasm did not blind Gilman to the problems of cities. Even in Herland, the density of population dramatically increased toward the center of the town. In practice, the City Beautiful often exacerbated urban problems, for the neighborhoods that bordered the well-planned parks, boulevards, and malls usually deteriorated. Even the area around the White City, after the close of the Exhibition in 1894, succumbed to this plague. "From the height of its Columbian Ecstacy," the architect Louis Sullivan wrote, "Chicago drooped and subsided with the rest, in a common sickness, the nausea of overstimulation."[2] As early as 1904, only four years after she settled in New York, Gilman proposed a solution to the problems of residential congestion. As usual, her social diagnosis was rooted in her own experience:

A ride on the Amsterdam Avenue streetcar in New York city will show the shanty and hovel of the ancient poor, and the crowded tenements of the modern poor; the large, comfortable, detached house of the ancient rich, with lawn and garden and outbuildings, and the long fronts of the side-street blocks where the "homes" stand like books on a shelf, squeezed out of all semblance of a house. This is due to the terrible constriction of financial pressure.

This pressure, relentlessly increasing, has forced upward from these level ranks of crowded dwellings the vertical outburst of the apartment-home— the "flat," and at this point begins most of the outcry.[3]

To relieve the pressure on available space, Gilman suggested, it was necessary to harness the forces of social evolution. The apartment-building was not a monstrous species of habitation, merely an inefficient one. Too much space is wasted, she averred, on individual heating plants, kitchens, and laundries. Better would it be to centralize all of these services. Better would it be to model all residential blocks on the apartment hotel, a self-contained community of unified construction with an inner court. "Once the precious laundry is surrendered," she explained, "the yard space could become an exquisite little park" complete "with vines and fountains, with delicious oriel windows, balconies, shaded corners, shrubs, and flowers. Or tennis courts could be laid out, and tether ball poles set up." Her recommendations may smack of naiveté; nevertheless, they suggest the extent to which Gilman still believed early in this century that fundamental urban reform was possible. Simply by rationalizing the delivery of a few domestic services, she thought, every family might "have a more reliable food supply at less cost; better heat and light at less cost; better air, more sun, a roof space for their own children, and far more beauty around them."[4] Unlike other reformers, who planned to relocate the urban poor in suburbs, Gilman hoped to renew the city in place.

Over the years, however, Gilman grew disillusioned with New York. The problems caused by congestion were severe and, like an advanced malignancy, resisted all methods of treatment. As Gilman concluded a poem, "The City of Death" (1913), written when she had lived in New York over a dozen years, she abhorred[5]

> A city whose own thick mephitic air
> Insidiously destroys its citizens;
> Whose buildings rob us of the blessed sun,
> The cleansing wind, the very breath of life;
> Whose weltering rush of swarming human forms,
> Forced hurtling through foul subterranean tubes
> Kills more than bodies, coarsens mind and soul.
> Destroys all grace and kindly courtesy,
> And steadily degrades our humanness
> To slavish acquiescence in its shame.

"Our Acromegous cities, breeders of disease and crime, degraders of humanity, impeders of progress, are the result of the malific force of competition," she added in 1916. "No natural force would ever lead a race of animals into conditions which are offensive to every sense," she added. A modern city is nothing more than "a great, dirty, crowded pen of human animals; ugly, clumsy, misgoverned; all too full of the sick and vicious and crazy results of its conditions; with a rate of civic infanticide only to be matched by its degrading effects on the children who survive." Gilman concluded that "children ought to grow up in the country, all of them."[6] She was especially disturbed by the "swarming human forms" of recent immigrants. Despite her xenophobia, she tolerated New York until 1922, as she later reminisced, having resided "Twenty-two years in that unnatural city where every one is an exile, none more so than the American." Unfortunately, "The petty minority of Americans in New York receive[s] small respect from [its] supplanters. . . . One of the bitterest lacks in that multiforeign city, that abnormally enlarged city, swollen rather than grown, is that of freedom in friendship and neighborliness."[7] "I increasingly hated New York and its swarms of jostling aliens," she wrote her old friend Alice Stone Blackwell. "The special gift of the different races are from three main causes: their stock, their environment, their culture. When transplanted to another environment, immersed in another culture, and mixed with another stock, their 'gifts' are lost!"[8] Her faith in the efficacy of specialization and social planning did not waver but, in her last years as a New Yorker, she shifted her allegiance from the overcrowded Nekropolis to the self-sufficient "new town" set in the country.

Her new proposals distinctly echo those of the English city planner Ebenezer Howard. Before the turn of the century, Howard had proposed to halt the growth of London and repopulate the rural districts with functional "garden cities" complete with light industry, schools, and theaters, enveloped in turn by green belts for farming. The concept was extremely influential in the 1920s and 1930s, especially among the decentrist school of city planners and urban reformers in this country, including Lewis Mumford. Gilman anticipated the popularity of Howard's ideas as early as 1913. With improved modes of modern transportation, "the swollen city, packed to bursting, foul, ugly, and dangerous," might be replaced by "loose-linked, wide-lying chain-cities, radiating like snow crystals, connected by rings and spokes of traffic lines."[9] She elaborated this scheme in two essays published in 1920 and 1921. In the first, she designed her own ideal "new town." "Applepieville," as she called her planned community, consisted of perhaps a hundred homes and farms organized around a social nucleus—a design, she argued, that would improve agricultural productivity and, more importantly, ease the burden on women: "With organization, specialization, and proper mechanical appliances, twenty or twenty-five women could do the cooking, the cleaning, laundry work, sewing and mending, and nursery-governessing that is now done by a hundred, and do it in an eight hour day. This would leave seventy-five to specialize in other work, to raise vegetables and small fruits" and so forth. To be sure, such a plan preserved conventional sex-roles, but its net effect, according to Gilman, would be "stronger, happier mothers, better education for little children, a pleasant and stimulating social life, and a larger income" for each family.[10] Similarly, in an essay the next year entitled "Making Towns Fit to Live in," she explained the advantages of planned industrial communities of perhaps a thousand persons—socialized company towns, as it were, in which basic domestic services would be supplied by specialists.[11]

Gilman wrote these essays, significantly enough, even as she and her husband were planning to abandon Manhattan for Norwich Town, Connecticut, where they settled in 1922. "After New York it is like heaven," she declared in her memoirs. "The people I meet, and mostly those I see in the neighborhood, are of native stock." Like the women in "Applepieville," she began to grow vegetables, some thirty varieties in a plot of nine thousand square feet (L, 326–27). "I'm well, happy, and vigorously at work in my garden," she wrote Blackwell in June 1925. "I never had a garden before, and I love it— madly! You should see me Dig! and Hoe! and Rake! And all the other things—numberless—there are to do in a garden."[12] Like Candide, her search for the best of all possible worlds ended in her garden, a single acre of land untainted by the miasma of the city.

His Religion and Hers

In late 1923, the year after she retired to Connecticut, Gilman published her final social treatise under the title His Religion and Hers. She again preached in it a sanguine faith in evolution, though she now allowed it would "be generations yet before women can cease to depend on men" (HRH, 278). Like Elizabeth Cady Stanton in the Woman's Bible nearly thirty years before, Gilman argued in the essay that traditional religions are morbid and male-oriented, formulated by hunters and fighters and thus erected upon the fear of death and hope for afterlife. She repudiated creeds devoted to personal immortality and she expected that, like government and the home, the religious institution would be refined through "a normal feminine influence" (HRH, 6). Religion, she asserted, "is the strongest help in modifying our conscious behavior" (HRH, 275). Whereas past patriarchal religions have effectively sanctioned patriarchal models of social organization,

The new premises for our religious thought will as inevitably lead to right conduct as the old premises have led to wrong. Where the older religions left life on earth neglected, the new will find its place of action here. Where the old saw human labor as a curse, the new will find in it joyful and natural expression of power. Where the old demanded belief in the unprovable and supernatural, the new will develop understanding of clear natural law. Where the old issued commands, the new will show cause and effect. Where the old drove the unwilling by threats of punishment, or lured them by promise of reward, the new will cultivate the natural powers which lead and push us on. Where the old saw life as evil and humanity as a broken, feeble thing, the new will see life as a glory, and humanity as its highest crown, rich with untested powers. (*HRH*, 260)

Gilman invoked no visions of heavenly pie-in-the-sky, but an earthly millennium realized through social progress: "We are so long-sighted in our passionate desire for an eternal existence in the other life, so short-sighted in our indifference to the really respectable number of millions of years before us in this one!" (*HRH*, 32). Her friend Alexander Black concluded that Gilman saw "man's religion as based upon a postponed heaven; woman's religion as expressing a desire for a heaven here and now." She saw "heaven not as a place, but as a race condition."[13]

Gilman's treatise was, for the most part, but a belabored recapitulation of her earlier work. As in *Human Work*, she presumed that people need not be prodded to contribute to the general welfare and appealed for "social experts" to manage the economy in lieu of the "social parasites who neither produce nor distribute" but skim personal profit (*HRH*, 269, 281). As in *The Man-Made World*, she distinguished between the "tendencies of the male sex" which "are often inimical to social progress" and "the tendencies of motherhood" which "are in line with social progress" (*HRH*, 48). For substantiation, she again cited Ward's chapter in *Pure Sociology* on the phylogenetic forces (*HRH*, 57). She echoed her argument, first and most fully elaborated in *Women and Economics*, that women have unfortunately submitted "to traditions and conventions forced upon them in the past" (*HRH*, 95). She lamented the unnatural modern relation of men and women: "By the early and universal subjection of the female to the male, by her segregation to the lowest form of service and to an exaggerated sex-development, we have made ourselves a crippled race, a race whose whole development was left to be carried on by one half of it" (*HRH*, 202–3). As in her essays for the *Forerunner*, she anticipated that fully enfranchised women "will be able to exercise an unmeasured influence to maintain peace." She thought war would "gradually disappear when an international motherhood takes the steps, so clearly possible, to protect the children of the world" (HRH, 259, 262).

Gilman also elaborated, in a more strident tone, her earlier objections to sexual license. She had long expected that, as women improved their status, they would progressively de-emphasize their sexual characteristics. Instead, as she noted with alarm, by the 1920s women were more sexually indulgent, like men of earlier generations. Gilman was dismayed by the growing popularity of Freudian theory among the sexual revolutionaries of the postwar period and, later, she would disparage psychoanalysts as "mind-meddlers" who had "read certain utterly unproven books" in order to "extract confessions of the last intimacy" from their patients (L, 314). Sexual liberation seemed to her a particularly nefarious modern rationalization for the sexual exploitation of women. "We now see advanced the theory that it is repression which ails us," she protested, and "that all that is needed to restore us to normality is for women to go as far wrong as men" (HRH, 65). She compared the "perverted sex-philosophy of Freud and his followers" to the phallic worship of ancient religions and dismissed it as a "species of biological blasphemy" (HRH, 165–66, 170). She anticipated, not the restoration of a primeval period of unrepressed Eros, but a future era when the sex function would be exercised primarily for procreational purposes. In later years, Gilman often reiterated her opposition to the sexual norm. People need to become "less sex crazy than at present, and capable of rational continence when it is necessary," she wrote in 1927.[14] "We must disabuse our minds of that mire of psycho-sexual theory which is directly responsible for so much of present day perversion," she added in 1929.[15] "It will take several generations of progressive selection, with widely different cultural influences, to reestablish a normal sex development in genus homo, with its consequences in happier marriage, better children, and wide improvement in the public health," she regretfully concluded in 1930.[16]

Reviewers of His Religion and Hers, while generally sympathetic, usually expressed only qualified praise. Gilman attributed its mixed reception to the unpopularity of her unfashionable opinions: Though the book "seemed to me rather a useful and timely work," she wrote in her memoirs, "unfortunately my views on the sex question do not appeal at all to the Freudian complex of to-day; nor are people satisfied with a presentation of religion as a help in our tremendous work of improving this world—what they want is hope of another world, with no work in it" (*L, 327*). In the *Birth Control Review*, William Pepperell Montague of Columbia University applauded Gilman's essay but admitted that her condemnation "as abnormal and excessive any use of the sex function except for procreation" was likely "to be offensive not only to readers of this magazine but to progressive-minded folk generally."[17] Hildegarde Fillmore in the *Bookman* admitted Gilman's analysis smacked of idealism, though she seemed more impatient than impractical.[18] The sociologist Edward Ross wrote the author that he thought *His Religion and Hers* a "wonderful book," though he added he did not "know how it will jibe with the vast and overwhelming array of facts as to early religions which the folklorists have brought together."[19] Amy Wellington in the *Literary Review* predicted that, while orthodox and ultramasculine readers "will not like the book," more "thoughtful men and women will welcome it and ponder."[20] Readers for the *Freeman* and the *Catholic Tribune* complained, respectively, that Gilman's wit seemed over the years "to have become a trifle acerbic, even a trifle hysterical" and her proposed religion was nothing less than "a return to and a revival of paganism." For better or worse, these were among the last reviews of her work Charlotte Perkins Gilman would read. All of her books were out-of-print by 1930, when the Century Company offered to sell her the plates to *His Religion and Hers* for only fifty dollars.[21]

Final Years

"I am sixty-four years old," Gilman noted one day late in 1924. "Practically I have done: a shelf of books—some of importance; a mass of magazine stuff—all tending upward; Poems—some excellent, some useful, none deleterious; Lectures—for thirty-four years—thousands I guess . . . . all tending upward. I ought to be at work ten more years."[22] The estimate of her longevity was prophetic. During the final decade of her life, though apparently reconciled to the slow eclipse of her reputation after her retirement, Gilman in fact recurrently tried and failed to win and hold an audience. She published on assignment several essays reflecting on the rise of women and recent social progress; wrote an autobiography and a detective novel; and revised her old work on social ethics. Her friend Amy Wellington compiled a new edition of her verse. Apart from a few essays, however, the work she produced during these years either appeared posthumously, as in the case of the autobiography, or remains unpublished. She was, for all practical purposes, either ignored or forgotten.

Gilman struck no distinctively new notes in her final few published essays. Indeed, though she gave them such various titles as "Woman's Achievements Since the Franchise," "Sex and Race Progress," "Feminism and Social Progress," "Toward Monogamy," and "Parasitism and Civilized Vice," she reiterated the same basic points in most of them. On the one hand, she was pleased to report that women were increasingly employed in remunerative work outside the home. "Married or single," she wrote in 1927, "women are becoming more numerous in industry."[23] On the other hand, many economically independent women, like newly manumitted slaves, had acquired vulgar tastes from the master class of men: "Just as women have imitated the drug-habits of men, without the faintest excuse or reason, merely to show that they can, so are they imitating men's sex habits, in large measure."[24] Still, Gilman was confident the corrupting influence of men on women's sexual mores "will not last long," perhaps only a few generations.[25]

By 1925, she had completed all but the brief final chapter of an autobiography, *The Living of Charlotte Perkins Gilman.* "We should not say 'life' as a noun but 'living' as an active verb," she had written, as if to explain the title (*HRH*, 98). The autobiography was an account of her formative years and her public career, her own record of political struggle with little regard to personal achievement. By design, the autobiography contains few glimpses of the private person, at least at the height of her reputation. Houghton Gilman, for example, is hardly mentioned. "It has been obvious for some time that Gilman did not tell all," Millicent Bell allows, and "that a true story of the life would show a personality even more conflicted and complex than she admitted."[26] According to Patricia Meyer Spacks, the autobiography betrays the author's anger and acute frustration, especially late in life. Gilman expressed "no distinct positive sense of personal identity," Spacks explains, but "denied the implicit egotism of autobiography by insisting that self is less important than service." Like the adolescent who had repressed her fantasy life to win her mother's approval, Gilman in her memoirs "subordinates her desire for distinction to her commitment to large causes and achieves greatly as a mysterious corollary to self-deprecation." Disguising "her anger by her insistent claims to selflessness," Gilman presented herself to the reader "as guide, even savior" with a compulsive need to serve humanity.[27] In the final chapter, written only a few weeks before her death in 1935, Gilman attempted to buffer her anger at her own irrelevance with hollow protests of happiness. When she offered to speak anywhere in Connecticut on behalf of the League of Women Voters, "the total result was one engagement in a neighboring town, audience of ten." She had hoped to be invited to lecture occasionally to students at the nearby Connecticut College for Women: "After so many years of work for the advancement of women, with a fairly world-wide reputation in that work, and with so much that was new and strong to say to the coming generation, it seemed to me a natural opportunity." Unfortunately, she added with undisguised pique, "It did not seem so to the college." She claimed, unconvincingly, that "My happiness was in Norwich" with her husband and "a few beloved friends," an assertion radically at odds with her self-portrayal in the active voice throughout her memoirs as a whole (*L,* 332–33). She finally placed the autobiography, with a foreword by her friend Zona Gale, with Appleton-Century in June 1935 with publication scheduled for October. Most early readers considered the work a valuable record of a remarkable life, as Dorothy Canfield observed in her review, "told with restraint, good taste, dignity, and a vivid warmth."[28] Spacks concludes more recently, with good reason, that "Gilman's life story is a paradigm of feminine anger."[29]

In the late 1920s, Gilman turned from nonfiction to experiment with "a species of detective story, at least unique" to the genre, whatever its other liabilities (*L,* 332). She had enjoyed detective fiction for years, especially Arthur Conan Doyle's tales of Sherlock Holmes, though she had criticized the classical formula for emphasizing plot at the expense of characterization.[30] She apparently designed her own detective novel, entitled *Unpunished,* to redress the imbalance. Her soft-boiled detectives, Jim and Bessie Hunt, investigate the death of Wade Vaughn, a local attorney celebrated for public benefaction who has apparently been dispatched in a case of extreme overkill: His body is found with a bullet hole in the temple, a long bruise on the head, a knife in and a cord around the neck, and a decanter of poisoned whiskey and an empty glass at hand. The prime suspect, his sister-in-law Jacqueline Warner, widowed and scarred by a car accident years before, Bessie declares "one of the most wonderful women I ever saw."[31] The Hunts discover, moreover, that Vaughn, "this prominent successful lawyer, this man hitherto supposed to have been so benevolently supporting three dependents," is in fact a blackmailer, a

misogynist, the most tyrannical male and unqualified villain in the
Gilman canon. He has driven his wife to suicide and insisted that
Jacqueline, her sister, submit to his every demand. "Here is this
woman, widowed, crippled, disinherited, disfigured, and the only
person on earth to look out for those two children," Bessie Hunt ex-
claims. "Even if she could have escaped with them any sort of court
would have given them back to him—what could she bring against
him—that would hold?" Like the narrator of "The Yellow Wall-paper," Jacqueline has kept a secret diary in which she has documented
Vaughn's fiendish crimes. Dozens of people have cause to kill him.
Ann J. Lane has observed that such dark intrigue may suggest "the
frustration [Gilman] experienced at having devoted a life to struggling for change that did not occur."[32] At an inquest, as it happens,
the coroner testifies that Vaughn died of heart disease, and thus no
one is charged with his murder. Later, Jacqueline reveals she scared
him to death by appearing in his presence wearing her sister's death
mask. Gilman left no doubt, however, that her action is morally jus-
tifiable. Jacqueline is not only "unpunished," as the title indicates,
but rewarded with plastic surgery which restores her features and
with marriage to the family doctor. Though a reader for a publisher
to whom she submitted the manuscript thought her characters "interesting," Gilman's plot construction was slipshod and her dialogue
stilted, and she predictably failed to place the story.

She had no more success in placing her revised *A Study in Ethics*
with a publisher. During the last months of her life she submitted a
draft to at least six publishing firms, including Viking, Macmillan,
Harcourt, and Harper, in each case to no avail. She was disappointed,
but not discouraged, her faith in the merit of the work unshaken. She
reread the essay in the spring of 1932 "with a view of revision" only
to conclude that "I cannot better it. It is social philosophy, well rea-
soned and clearly connected, and save for illustrations it *has no date—*
at least as long as we remain in our present stage of economic development." If she could not place the work with a publisher, "if I can
do no more while alive I mean to place [copies of the manuscript] in
some public libraries and universities."[33] In October 1930, at the age
of seventy, Gilman mourned her lost popularity in a letter to Alice
Stone Blackwell: "I'm not writing much now. Have failed to place
my last three books—a very poor autobiography, a book on ethics,
and a story. These very young readers, editors, & critics have no use
for writers over thirty."[34] Two months later, she again wrote Black-

well that "I greatly miss my audience—no lectures wanted anymore, and books not taken."[35] She no longer had even the urge to write, she admitted, else "I could lay up mss. for posthumous publication."[36]

Her health was good, in some respects better than in years, until the final months of her life. As she wrote Blackwell in January 1928, "I'm well, better in spirits and working power than for ever and ever so long. I can read more than since the big breakdown in 1885–86."[37] In 1930, she noted she had turned "Seventy. What of it?" In 1931, she observed that, despite her advancing age, she enjoyed excellent health: "Nothing the matter with me."[38] In January 1932, however, she learned that she had inoperable breast cancer. "I had not the least objection to dying," she wrote, "but I did not propose to die of this, so I promptly bought sufficient chloroform as a substitute" (*L,* 333). Her "only distress was for Houghton" (*L,* 333), who died unexpectedly from a cerebral hemorrhage in May 1934: "34 years of happiness we had together—that is enough to be thankful for," she wrote a friend.[39] "Whatever I felt of loss and pain was outweighed by gratitude for an instant, painless death for him. She was relieved "that he did not have to see me wither and die—and he be left alone" (*L,* 334). She flew to Pasadena, her old home, in the fall of 1934 to be near her family, there to be joined by Grace Channing, now a widow. "I am most unconcernedly willing to die when I am ready," she wrote in her final days. She had "no faintest belief in personal immortality" as defined by orthodox creed. Instead she explained, "My life is in humanity—and that goes on" (*L,* 335). In the end, she comforted her friends by quoting from section 48 of Whitman's "Song of Myself': "No words can say how utterly at peace I am about God and about death."[40]

As her disease advanced, Gilman chose to end her life rather than suffer for no reason. Her suicide was carefully premeditated. Years earlier, while in Oakland, as her mother lay dying of cancer, she had told Harriet Howe that "If this should come to me, in future years, I will *not* go through with it. It is needless."[41] Incredibly, over twenty-three years before her death, Gilman described in an essay published in the *Forerunner* the exact manner in which she would exercise the right to die:

The neatest suicide I ever heard of was that of a well-bred New England woman, who, for reasons of her own, wished to "discontinue." She waited till Saturday evening, "tub-night," as they used to call it. Everything in the house was in order and as clean as a new pin. She took a bath, arranged herself in a clean, fresh nightie, and calmly went to bed. In a large newspaper cone she placed a crumpled towel, poured in a bottle of chloroform, and inverted the cone over face. Washed and straightened, hands folded on her breast, she was found there, no trouble to anyone.[42]

On Saturday, 17 August 1935, Charlotte Perkins Gilman ended her life as she had planned—in bed, after her bath, with cloths soaked in chloroform over her face.[43] She left a typed note, an excerpt from the valedictory chapter of her memoirs, in which she specified two criteria of rational suicide: "When all usefulness is over, when one is assured of imminent death, it is the simplest of human rights to choose a quick and easy death in place of a slow and horrible one" (L, 333). Gilman justified her final act on utilitarian grounds: She was no longer able to serve humanity and she preferred chloroform to cancer. By the manner of her death, significantly, she again commanded public attention. Her suicide was, in a sense, her final public statement, her suicide note the last piece she prepared for publication. During the ensuing controversy over the right to die, both Carrie Chapman Catt and the novelist Fannie Hurst rallied to her defense. Hurst asserted, as if in epitaph, "She was a wise woman. She died as wisely as she lived."[44]

At her death, Gilman was virtually forgotten despite her early reputation as an astute social critic. In 1922, Catt had ranked her first among twelve prominent American women, crediting her books "with utterly revolutionizing the attitude of mind in the entire country, indeed of other countries, as to woman's place."[45] In the spring of 1935, Catt reassured Gilman that "You leave behind an influence too great to measure."[46] In 1940, she reiterated in a letter to Katharine Stetson Chamberlain that "Your mother's ideas were taken up and used by speakers and writers everywhere," though she implicitly acknowledged in her next sentence that her mother had not received due credit for her contributions: "I dare say the average worker of that time failed to realize how much the movement owed to Mrs. Gilman."[47] In 1956, a generation after her death, Carl N. Degler observed that Gilman "has suffered a neglect in American intellectual history difficult to explain." Degler began to correct the oversight by publishing the first modern scholarly estimate of her work. "If, as most would agree, America in the last fifty years has basically altered its attitude toward the working woman," he concluded, "then Charlotte Perkins Gilman must be assigned a significant part in the accomplishment of that change."[48]

With the revival of feminism in the 1960s, Gilman was literally rediscovered. She seemed to have anticipated, by word and example, latter-day struggles for the social and economic liberation of women. Over the past few years all of her major works have been reprinted. Her papers, formerly in the possession of her daughter Katharine, were acquired in 1971–72 by the Schlesinger Library at Radcliffe College and reproduced on over six hundred microfiche for use by scholars. Ironically, her life and works are more accessible, her character and accomplishments more easily gauged now than ever before. More than any other American of her generation, Charlotte Perkins Gilman despised the home that imprisoned wife and child and called for its reformation. Her legacy is greater than many another whose name is better known. "The immortality I believe in is for the race, for our continuing ascending humanity," she wrote Alice Stone Blackwell a few months before her death. "To that progress you and I and the others have contributed, in it we live."[49]

Abbreviations

The following abbreviations are used in the notes to specify the locations of primary, usually manuscript, material:

CPG Papers Charlotte Perkins Gilman Papers, Radcliffe College

HU Houghton Library, Harvard University

IU Lilly Library, Indiana University

LC Manuscript Division, Library of Congress

NAWSA National American Women Suffrage Association Records

RIHS Rhode Island Historical Society, Providence, Rhode Island

SC Smith College, Northampton, Massachusetts

WC Wagner College, Staten Island, New York

The following abbreviations are used in the notes and parenthetically within the text to cite specific editions of Gilman's works:

CPGR *The Charlotte Perkins Gilman Reader* (New York, 1980)

CC *Concerning Children* (Boston, 1900)

Hrld *Herland* (New York, 1979)

HRH *His Religion and Hers* (New York, 1923)

H *The Home* (New York, 1903)

HW *Human Work* (New York, 1904)

ITOW *In This Our World* (Boston, 1898)

L *The Living of Charlotte Perkins Gilman* (New York, 1935)

MMW *The Man-Made World* (New York, 1911)

W&E *Women and Economics* (Boston, 1898)

Notes and References

Preface

1. "Foreword" to *L*, xxxvii.
2. *Forerunner* 7 (January 1916);56.
3. *Forerunner* 4 (February 1913):36; *Visual Review* 1 (1926):2; Alexander Black, "The Woman Who Saw It First," *Century* 107 (November 1923):42; Ann J. Lane, introduction to *CPGR,* xiv.

Chapter One

1. CPG to Schmalhausen, 28 July 1930, folder 122, CPG Papers.
2. Mary A. Hill, *Charlotte Perkins Gilman: The Making of a Radical Feminist 1860–1896* (Philadelphia, 1980),13.
3. *Forerunner* 2 (July 1911);196–97
4. CAP to Martha Luther, 29 July 1881, RIHS.
5. Diary, 30 March 1880, vol. 17, CPG Papers.
6. CPS to Martha Luther Lane, 27 July 1890, RIHS.
7. CAP to Martha Luther, 1 August 1881, RIHS.
8. CAP to Martha Luther, 8 and 16 August 1881, RIHS.
9. CAP to CWS, 13 February 1882, folder 39, CPG Papers.
10. CAP to CWS, 20 February 1882, folder 39, CPG Papers.
11. CAP to CWS, 21 February 1882, folder 39, CPG Papers.
12. Carol Berkin, "Private Woman, Public Woman," in *Women in America* (Boston, 1979),158.
13. CAP to CWS, 20 February 1882, folder 39, CPG Papers.
14. Hill, *Charlotte Perkins Gilman,* 119.
15. Diary, 9 May 1884, vol. 19, CPG Papers.
16. Diary, 30 August 1885, vol. 19, CPG Papers.
17. Ibid.
18. CPS to Martha Luther Lane, 4 January 1886, RIHS.
19. Diary, 5 and 19 January 1887, vol. 20, CPG Papers.
20. Ann Douglas, *Journal of Interdisciplinary History* 4 (Summer 1973):41–44.
21. CPS to Martha Luther Lane, 4 January 1886, RIHS.
22. *Pacific Monthly* 1(October 1889):43;2 (September 1890):177.
23. CPS to Martha Luther Lane, 20 January and 27 July 1890, RIHS. CPS was also disappointed by Howells's farce *The Mouse-Trap* (diary, 5 January 1887, vol. 19, CPG Papers).
24. *Land of Sunshine* 12 (May 1900):348.
25. *Forerunner* 2 (July 1911):197; *Impress* 1 (December 1893):5.

26. CPS to Martha Luther Lane, 27 July 1890, RIHS; Elaine Showalter, *A Literature of Their Own* (Princeton: Princeton University Press, 1977), 198–201.

27. "Our Opportunity," folder 164, CPG Papers; diary, 8 April and 25 May 1891, vol. 30; 10 December 1897, vol. 36; and 1 March 1898, vol. 38, CPG Papers; Harriet Howe, "Charlotte Perkins Gilman—As I Knew Her," *Equal Rights,* 5 September 1936, 212.

28. *Forerunner* 2 (July 1911):197.

29. *Pacific Monthly* 3 (May 1891):194–98.

30. Diary, 11 March 1890, vol. 29 CPG Papers; *New England Magazine,* n.s. 4 (June 1891):480–85.

31. Folder 260 and vol. 23, CPG Papers. This story was twice published, in *Kate's Field's Washington* in 1890 and in the *Forerunner* 4 (November 1913):281–84.

32. Folder 260 and vol. 23, CPG Papers. This story was twice published, in *Kate Field's Washington* in 1890 and in the *Forerunner* 4, (December 1913):309–13.

33. Folders 214–15, CPG Papers.

34. *L,* 112; diary, 3 and 5 February 1898, vol. 38, CPG Papers.

35. CPS to Martha Luther Lane, 15 August 1889, RIHS.

36. CPS to Martha Luther Lane, 22 October 1889 and 20 January 1890, RIHS.

37. CPG to Howells, 17 October 1919, HU.

38. Sandra Gilbert and Susan Gubar, *The Madwoman in the Attic* (New Haven, 1979), 90.

39. CPS to Martha Luther Lane, 27 July 1890, RIHS; diary, 21 March 1887, vol. 20, CPG Papers.

40. *Boston Transcript,* 1 January 1892, 6, col. 5.

41. "A Reminiscent Introduction" to *Great Modern American Stories* (New York: Boni and Liveright, 1920),vii.

42. *Conservator* 10 (June 1899):60–61; *Forerunner* 1 (December 1910):33.

43. *Boston Transcript,* 8 April 1892, 6, col. 2.

44. CPG to W. D. Howells, 17 October 1919, HU.

45. Howells to CPG, 7 October 1919, folder 120, CPG Papers.

46. CPG to Howells, 17 October 1919, HU.

47. Elaine Hedges, "Afterword" to *The Yellow Wall-paper* (Old Westbury, 1973),37.

48. Mary A. Hill, *Massachusetts Review* 21 (1980):512.

49. Annette Kolodny, *New Literary History* 11 (Spring 1980):457.

50. Hedges, "Afterword,"41.

51. Jean Kennard, *New Literary History* 13 (Autumn 1981):76–77.

52. Vol. 29, CPG Papers.

53. *American Fabian* 2 (January 1897):12.

54. "Gilman, Charlotte Perkins Stetson," in *DAB* (1944).

55. Anne Firor Scott, *Reviews in American History* 8 (December 1980):446.

56. Hill, *Charlotte Perkins Gilman,* pp. 170–85.

57. Edward Bellamy, *Looking Backward 2000–1887* (Boston: Houghton Mifflin, 1966),72–73, 157.

58. *New Nation,* 28 March 1891, 139.

59. CPS to Martha Luther Lane, 15 April 1890, RIHS.

60. CPS to Martha Luther Lane, 15 March 1890, RIHS.

61. Vol. 23, CPG Papers.

62. *L,* 113; folder 120, CPG Papers.

63. CPS to Howells, 16 June 1890, HU.

64. *L,* 129; folder 36, CPG Papers.

65. *Cosmopolitan* 10 (January 1891):272.

66. *Nationalist* 3 (February 1891):491.

67. *American Journal of Sociology* 2 (May 1897):815; *Glimpses of the Cosmos* (New York: G.P. Putnam's Sons, 1917), 5:336–40.

68. *San Francisco Examiner,* 4 February 1894, 6:4–5.

69. Vol. 29, CPG Papers.

70. Folder 163 and vol. 29, CPG Papers.

71. *Weekly Nationalist,* 21 June 1890, 6.

72. CPS to Martha Luther Lane, 27 July 1890, RIHS.

73. Howe, "Charlotte Perkins Gilman," 211.

74. *Weekly Nationalist,* 26 July 1890, 4–5; folder 168, CPG Papers.

75. Folder 168, CPG Papers.

76. "Our Opportunity," folder 164, CPG Papers.

77. Folder 165, CPG Papers.

78. Folder 164, CPG Papers.

79. "An Unmarried Child," folders 168–69, CPG Papers.

80. Folder 164, CPG Papers.

81. "Social, Cosmetic and Human Life," folder 165, CPG Papers. By prescribing monogamy as the *present* ideal, CPS held open the possibility that the evolution of the species would one day permit a wider range of ideal relationships, a view shared by her aunt Isabella Beecher Hooker.

82. "Nationalism and the Virtues," folder 163, CPG Papers.

83. *Los Angeles Porcupine,* 1 January 1891, oversize vol. 3, CPG Papers.

84. *New Nation,* 31 May 1891, 259.

85. *New Nation,* 6 June 1891, 307.

86. "What is Nationalism?" folder 168, CPG Papers.

87. Vols. 30–31, CPG Papers.

88. *New Nation,* 23 January 1892, 58.

89. Folder 168, CPG Papers.

90. Diary, 15 January 1892, vol. 31, CPG Papers.

91. CPS to Edwin Markham, 19 January 1892, WC.

92. *Forerunner* 2 (February 1911):31–36.

93. Vol. 31, CPG Papers.

94. Bellamy to CPS, 19 February 1891, folder 137, CPG Papers.

95. Carol Farley Kessler, *Regionalism and the Female Imagination* 4 (Winter 1979):35.

96. *New Nation,* 24 June 1893, 315.

97. Bellamy to CPS, 14 January 1894, folder 137, CPG Papers.

98. *Impress* 1 (April 1894):6; vol. 2, CPG Papers.

99. Howe, "Charlotte Perkins Gilman," 211.

100. CPS to Edwin Markham, 28 March 1892, WC.

101. Vol. 31, CPG Papers.

102. *Boston Globe,* 17 December 1892, folder 282, CPG Papers.

103. *Boston Herald,* 20 December 1892, folder 282, CPG Papers.

104. *New Nation,* 24 June 1893, 315.

105. *Impress* 1 (November 1893):2; (December 1893):1; vol. 2, CPG Papers.

106. *Impress,* 5 January 1895, 4–5; vol. 2, CPG Papers.

107. *Impress,* 12 January 1895, 3; vol. 2, CPG Papers. As late as 1907, CPG explained that *Looking Backward* had enjoyed enormous popularity because it "has scarce a feature beyond the grasp of the average citizen" (*Times* 1 [January 1907];215).

108. *Impress,* 19 January 1895; vol. 2, CPG Papers.

109. Diary, 7 June 1898, vol. 38, CPG Papers.

110. *W&E,* 242–44; *H,* 132–33. In *The Home,* according to one contemporary critic, Gilman arranged the "domesticities . . . somewhat after the fashion of 'Looking Backward' " (*New York Times Saturday Review of Books,* 26 December 1903, 983). See also Dolores Hayden, "Charlotte Perkins Gilman and the Kitchenless House," *Radical History Review* 21 (Fall 1979):227–29.

Chapter Two

1. Howe, "Charlotte Perkins Gilman," 214.

2. CPS to Edwin Markham, 20 February 1894, WC.

3. *Worthington's Illustrated Magazine* 1 (May 1893):453–59.

4. Diary, 21 September 1890, vol. 29, CPG Papers.

5. Diary, 17 June 1893, vol. 32, CPG Papers; *Impress,* 16 February 1895, 4–5; *Forerunner* 4 (June 1913):141–43; 7 (November 1916):281–85.

6. *Forerunner* 6 (July 1915):174; 7(July 1916):157.

7. Quoted in Hill, *Charlotte Perkins Gilman,* 234.

8. *Impress,* 17 November 1894, 5.

9. CPS to GHG, 20 January 1900, folder 79, CPG Papers.

10. *American Journal of Sociology* 12 (March 1907):713–14.

11. Diary, 1 September 1885, vol. 19; 18 October 1898, vol. 37, CPG Papers.

12. *Impress,* 15 December 1894, 15.
13. Howe, "Charlotte Perkins Gilman," 215.
14. Floyd Dell, *Women as World Builders* (Chicago, 1913), 24.
15. *Overland Monthly* n.s. 23 (May 1894):555; quoted in *Impress,* 17 November 1894, 10.
16. Vol. 34, CPG Papers.
17. Unless otherwise noted, all reviews of *ITOW* cited in this section may be located in folder 298, CPG Papers.
18. *Dial,* 1 September 1898, 134.
19. *Literature,* 17 January 1899, 43; *Current Literature* 25 (February 1899):115–16.
20. *Land of Sunshine* 3 (October 1895):239; 9 (September 1898):201; 11 (July 1899):118.
21. *Topeka State Journal,* 15 June 1896, vol. 7, CPG Papers.
22. *Bookman* 8 (September 1898):51.
23. Diary, 3 September 1898, vol. 38, CPG Papers.
24. *Poet-lore* 11 (January 1899):128.
25. *Athenaeum,* 30 December 1899, 893.
26. Diary, 5 April 1883, vol. 18, CPG Papers.
27. "Beginners," folder 165, CPG Papers.
28. "Owning Things," folder 165, CPG Papers; diary, 10 August 1891, vol. 29, CPG Papers.
29. Diary, 14 May 1897, vol. 36, CPG Papers; *ITOW,* 94.
30. *Forerunner* 2 (July 1911):197; diary, 10 November 1897, vol. 36, CPG Papers.
31. Diary, 5 December 1897, vol. 36, CPG Papers.
32. *HW,* 102, 305; *Forerunner* 6 (December 1915):326; *New York Times,* 1 June 1921, 16, col. 7.
33. *Conservator* 9 (September 1898):109.
34. Diary, 19 October 1898, vol. 38, CPG Papers.
35. Howells to CPS, 19 December 1891, folder 120, CPG Papers.
36. Howells to CPS, 11 July 1894, folder 120, CPG Papers.
37. *Harper's Weekly,* 25 January 1896, 79; *North American Review* 168 (May 1899):589–90.
38. Diary, 20 March and 8 December 1897, vol. 36, CPG Papers.
39. Howells to CPG, 8 May 1911, folder 120, CPG Papers.
40. CPS to GHG, 20 and 23 October 1898, folder 57, CPG Papers.
41. Howe, "Charlotte Perkins Gilman," 215.
42. "The Social Service Bureau," folder 174, CPG Papers.
43. Diary, 31 January 1896, vol. 35, CPG Papers.
44. Diary, 23 January 1896, vol. 35, CPG Papers.
45. *Forerunner* 4 (June 1913):165.
46. *Woman's Journal,* 1 February 1896, 36.
47. *Pure Sociology* (New York: Macmillan 1903), 325.
48. Vol. 7, CPG Papers; *New Nation,* 22 April 1893, 204.

49. *Impress* 1 (June 1894):1.

50. *Forum* 6 (November 1888):275.

51. Ward to CPS, 28 December 1895, 17 January 1896, folder 124; and diary, 23 and 28 January 1896, vol. 35, CPG Papers.

52. *Forerunner* 4 (June 1913):166; 1 (October 1910):26–27.

53. *Forerunner* 4 (June 1913):166.

54. *Amerikanische Turnzeitung,* 8 December 1935, 9.

55. Diary, 28 July 1896, vol. 35, CPG Papers.

56. *Current Literature* 25 (February 1899):115.

57. CPS to Howells, 6 April 1897, HU.

58. *American Fabian* 2 (January 1897):9–12; 3 (June 1897):2–3; 4 (March 1898):6–7; 3 (August 1897):6.

59. *Impress* 3 November 1894, 10.

60. *Forerunner* 3 (June 1912):167.

61. Diary, 9 May 1897, vol. 36, CPG Papers.

62. Diary, 1 July 1897, vol. 36, CPG Papers.

63. Diary, 19 July 1897, vol. 36, CPG Papers.

64. Diary, 30 November 1897, vol. 36, CPG Papers. See also Lois N. Magner, "Women and the Scientific Idiom," *Signs* 4 (Autumn 1978):68–77.

65. Diary, 5 October 1897, vol. 36, CPG Papers.

66. CPS to Mr. Garrison, 5 January 1898, SC.

67. *New York Times,* 26 February 1914, 9, col. 3.

68. *American Journal of Sociology* 14 (March 1909):618.

69. David Katzman, *Seven Days a Week* (New York: Oxford University Press, 1978), 284, 292.

70. Vol. 36, CPG Papers.

71. *Conservator* 9 (September 1898):110.

72. CPS to GHG, 22 May 1898, folder 51, CPG Papers.

73. Florence Kelley to CPS, 26 July 1898, folder 137, CPG Papers.

74. Joan Hedrick, *Solitary Comrade* (Chapel Hill: University of North Carolina Press, 1982), 134.

75. *Nation,* 8 June 1899, 443.

76. Diary, 19 June 1899, vol. 40, CPG Papers.

77. *Land of Sunshine* 11 (July 1899):118.

78. *Conservator* 9 (July 1898):76–77.

79. *Political Science Quarterly* 14 (December 1899):712–13.

80. *Dial,* 1 February 1899, 85–86.

81. *North American Review* 175 (July 1902):71–90.

82. *London Daily Chronicle,* 26 June 1899; folder 299, CPG Papers.

83. London *Bookman* 16 (September 1899):163–64.

84. Carl Degler, Introduction to *W&E* (New York, 1966), xiii.

85. T.V. Smith, *The American Philosophy of Equality* (Chicago: University of Chicago Press, 1927), 298.

86. Diary, 16 and 21 April 1899, vol. 40, CPG Papers.

87. *L,* 257–70; *Saturday Evening Post,* 27 May 1899, 758; *Arena* 22 (September 1899):342–50; *Ainslee's* 4 (September 1899):145–51. CPS readily allowed that her articles about the Congress were "extremely poor stuff . . . . With ease and freedom and some merit, I write thoughts, ideas, reasoning, yes, and feeling too, but descriptive work . . . . is beyond me" (*L,* 268).

Chapter Three

1. Diary, 12 August 1896, vol. 34, CPG Papers.
2. CPS to GHG, 16 May 1900, folder 84, CPG Papers.
3. CPS to GHG, 15 September 1898, folder 55, CPG Papers.
4. Diary, 11 June 1900, vol. 42, CPG Papers.
5. CPS to GHG, 6 May 1898, folder 50, CPG Papers.
6. Diary, 4 November and 14 December 1902, vol. 44, CPG Papers.
7. *Success* 11 (August 1908):490–91, 522–26. CPG later rewrote this story as a one-act play published in the *Forerunner* 2 (May 1911):115–23, 134.
8. *L,* 298–301; folders 7, 288–92, CPG Papers; *Booklovers* 4 (1904):385–90.
9. Black, "The Woman Who Saw It First," 39.
10. *Forerunner* 1 (January 1910):28; 2 (July 1911):169.
11. *L,* 294; *Current Literature* 36 (April 1904):388–89.
12. Vol. 24, CPG Papers.
13. Diary, 11 March 1899, vol. 40, CPG Papers.
14. *Cosmopolitan* 27 (October 1899):678 82.
15. *Land of Sunshine* 12 (March 1900):302.
16. Folder 230, CPG Papers; CPG to Benjamin Huebach, 1 March 1932, LC.
17. *Cosmopolitan* 37 (June 1904):170.
18. *Cosmopolitan* 27 (September 1899):477.
19. *Land of Sunshine* 12 (May 1900):349.
20. *HW,* 228. In her early essay "The Two Armies" (*Weekly Nationalist,* 28 June 1890, 6), CPS advocated the creation of an "industrial army" in which individualism is sacrificed to the social organism: "The industrial army would imply discipline, and temporary and willing subjection." Eventually, she hoped, the industrial army would wither away: "When men are wise enough to live in honesty, to take from the world no more than they put in it, to let a man have what he earns even if they are smart enough to get it away from him—then we can disband our industrial army, and live in peace indeed." CPS would strike the same authoritarian note often during her career. For example, she proposed, soon after the publication of *Human Work,* compulsory "enlistment" of most blacks in a CCC-like "army" similar to the industrial army of Nationalism (*American Journal of Sociology* 14 [July

1908]:78–85). See also *Forerunner* 4 (March 1913):80, where CPG credited "our own Bellamy" with recognizing in "his 'Industrial Army' " that economic processes are social processes.

21. Hayden, "Charlotte Perkins Gilman," 232.

22. Diary, 1 February and 17 November 1900, vol. 42, CPG Papers; *HW*, 72, 179, 219, 309; *H*, 194; *Forerunner* 3 (August 1912):217; 4 (July 1913):192; 5 (February 1914):52.

23. *Current Literature* 37 (October 1904):373–75.

24. Folder 304, CPG Papers; *Forerunner* 1 (December 1910):33.

25. *Atlantic Monthly* 94 (August 1904):274–75.

26. *Boston Evening Transcript*, 20 July 1904, 16, cols. 1–2.

27. Diary, 15 August 1900, vol. 42, CPG Papers.

28. *CC*, 9–14; *Hrld*, 78; *Forerunner* 1 (December 1910):10–11.

29. *MMW*, 203–4; *Hrld*, 69; *New York Times*, 5 March 1914, 8, col. 8; *North American Review* 224 (December 1927):622–29; *Nation*, 27 January 1932, 108–9.

30. *New York Times*, 19 March 1914, 8, col. 8.

31. *New York Times*, 25 May 1914, 11, col. 5.

32. *New York Tribune*, 26 February 1903, 7, col. 1.

33. *Forerunner* 1 (June 1910):12; 3 (March 1912):75.

34. *New York Times Saturday Review of Books*, 5 January 1901, 4.

35. *Forerunner* 1 (December 1910):33.

36. *Unity*, 9 May 1901, 155.

37. *Charities*, 1 February 1902, 120–21.

38. *Athenaeum*, 18 May 1901, 628–29.

39. *Women and Social Service* (Warren, Ohio, 1907), 11.

40. *Forerunner* 4 (November 1913):298; 7 (March 1916):83; *Hrld*, 106.

41. *Success* 12 (June 1909):370–71, 410–11.

42. *New York Tribune*, 12 March 1903, 7, col. 1.

43. *Puritan* 7 (December 1899):417–22.

44. William O'Neill, *Everyone Was Brave* (New York 1969), 44.

45. *New York Times*, 12 March 1914, 8, col. 8.

46. *H*, 131; *New York Tribune*, 7 April 1903, 7, col. 4.

47. *Independent*, 14 June 1906, 1401.

48. CPG to Upton Sinclair, 31 August 1910, IU.

49. *Annals of the American Academy* 48 (July 1913):94.

50. *American Journal of Sociology* 14 (March 1909):600–601; *New York Times*, 29 December 1908, 5:3; *Harper's Bazar*, 40 (June 1906):495–98.

51. *Harper's Bazar* 41 (July 1907):626–27.

52. *Forerunner* 1 (May 1910):15; 5 (June 1914):168; 7 (January 1916):23.

53. Folder 303, CPG Papers.

54. *Critic* 43 (December 1903):568–70.

55. *Current Literature* 37 (July 1904):42–43; *Dial,* 16 April 1904, 260–61; *Independent,* 7 January 1904, 40.

56. Walter Lippmann, *Drift and Mastery* (Englewood Cliffs: Prentice-Hall, 1961), 124.

57. Charles and Mary Beard, *The Rise of American Civilization* (New York: Macmillan, 1928), 2:431.

58. Hayden, "Charlotte Perkins Gilman," 225, 239.

59. *Forerunner* 1 (August 1910):13.

60. Hayden, "Charlotte Perkins Gilman," 241.

61. *Forerunner* 1 (October 1910):17.

62. Hayden, "Charlotte Perkins Gilman," 230.

63. *Survey,* 11 February 1911, 808.

64. *Independent,* 16 March 1911, 571.

65. *Academy,* 31 August 1912, 272.

66. *New York Times,* 2 April 1914, 11, cols. 1–2.

67. CPS to GHG, 10 and 22 July 1897, folder 43, CPG Papers.

68. CPS to GHG, 18 September 1897, folder 45, CPG Papers.

69. Diary, 2 December 1897, vol. 36, CPG Papers.

70. *New York Tribune,* 11 October 1903, 7, col. 4.

71. Ward to CPG, 9 February 1907, folder 124, CPG Papers.

72. *Independent,* 8 March 1906, 541.

73. *Forerunner* 1 (October 1910):26–27.

74. Ward to CPG, 11 February 1911, folder 124, CPG Papers.

75. Hill, *Charlotte Perkins Gilman,* 268.

76. *New York Times Review of Books,* 26 February 1911, 111; *Current Literature* 51 (July 1911):68.

77. *Literary Digest,* 22 April 1911, 796; *Independent,* 13 April 1911, 793.

78. *New York Times,* magazine sec., 15 January 1911, 14.

79. *A. L. A. Booklist* 7 (April 1911):330.

80. *Dial,* 16 June 1911, 471.

81. *Times* 1 (January 1907):215–20; 1 (February 1907):369–76; 1 (March 1907):498–504. Page proofs (591–97) of the April installment may be located in folder 260, CPG Papers.

82. Here Gilman once more betrayed Bellamy's influence. Street echos Julian West's exclamation, upon awakening in twenty-first-century Boston: "I really think that the complete absence of chimneys and their smoke is the detail that first impressed me" (Bellamy, *Looking Backward 2000–1887,* 25).

83. Arthur Vance to CPG, 30 October 1923, folder 123, CPG Papers.

Chapter Four

1. *Forerunner* 2 (October 1911):282.

2. CPG to Mabel Hay Mussey, 24 March 1909, HU.

3. *New York Times,* 19 February 1914, 9, col. 3; 26 February 1914,

9, col. 3; 5 March 1914, 8, col. 8; 12 March 1914, 8, col. 8;19 March 1914, 8, col. 8; 26 March 1914, 10, col. 8; 2 April 1914, 11, cols. 1–2; 9 April 1914, 10, col. 8.

4. CPG to Mabel Hay Mussey, 28 December 1910, HU.

5. CPG to Howells, 17 October 1919, HU.

6. *Forerunner* 1 (January 1910):29; 2 (January 1911):28.

7. *L,* 305; CPG to Tadaichi Okado, 30 June 1920, folder 239, CPG Papers.

8. Introduction to the *Forerunner* (New York: Greenwood Press, 1968), 1:iv.

9. Folder 239 and oversize vol. 3, CPG Papers.

10. Dell, *Women as World Builders,* 22; foreword to *L,* xxxii.

11. *Forerunner* 1 (December 1909):10; folder 311, CPG Papers; *The Cry for Justice,* ed. Upton Sinclair (Philadelphia: Winston, 1915), 662. Sinclair also described CPG as "America's most brilliant woman poet and critic" (200).

12. Mary Austin, *Earth Horizon* (Boston: Houghton Mifflin, 1932), 326.

13. Malcolm Cowley, "A Natural History of American Naturalism," in *Critiques and Essays on Modern Fiction* (New York: Ronald Press, 1952), 376.

14. Charles Walcutt, *American Literary Naturalism* (Minneapolis: University of Minnesota Press, 1956). p. 29.

15. Richard Hofstadter, *Social Darwinism in American Thought* (Boston: Beacon Press, 1955), 24.

16. Theodore Dreiser, *Newspaper Days* (New York: Liveright, 1931), 457.

17. Jack London, *Martin Eden* (New York: Macmillan, 1908), 108.

18. *Forerunner* 1 (November 1909):25.

19. *Forerunner* 2 (1911):52, 56, 79–80, 137, 165, 219, 278, 305, 307, and passim.

20. *Independent,* 21 March 1912, 630; *New York Times Review of Books,* 4 February 1912, 52, col. 3.

21. *Impress* 1 (November 1893):2.

22. "The Spirit of the Times in Art," folder 172, CPG Papers.

23. Bellamy, *Looking Backward,* 23, 25. Significantly, Morgan Street, the protagonist of Gilman's "A Woman's Utopia," had also echoed West's declaration upon landing in New York after an absence of twenty years.

24. Vol. 32, CPG Papers.

25. *Impress* 1 (December 1893):1.

26. *Forerunner* 6 (February 1915):53.

27. Hill, *Massachusetts Review,* 523.

28. *Forerunner* 7 (March 1916):83.

29. Howe, "Charlotte Perkins Gilman," 216; *Forerunner* 7 (May 1916):123.

30. *Forerunner* 7 (1916):125, 208, 291, 295, and passim.

31. Walcutt, *American Literary Naturalism*, 22; Philip Rahv, *Image and Idea* (New York: New Directions, 1949), 128–38.

32. *Forerunner* 6 (June 1915):141–45.

33. *L*, 290–91; diary, 17 December 1901, vol. 43; 14 January 1902, vol. 44, CPG Papers.

34. *Woman's World* 28 (March 1911):12–13, 58; reprint in *Forerunner* 7 (September 1916):225–32.

35. *Forerunner* 3 (February 1912):29–33.

36. *Forerunner* 3 (December 1912):309–14.

37. *Forerunner* 6 (September 1915):230–36.

38. Diary, 11 February 1902, vol. 44, CPG Papers; *L*, 93; *Forerunner* 7 (June 1916):146.

39. *Forerunner* 2 (1911):46, 72, 99, 158, 213, 239, and passim.

40. *Independent*, 21 March 1912, 629.

41. *Forerunner* 3 (1912):47, 324, and passim.

42. *Forerunner* 4 (1913):70, 207, and passim.

43. *Forerunner* 5 (1914):70 and passim.

44. *Forerunner* 6 (April 1915):101; 4 (May 1913):111–12.

45. *Forerunner* 6 (1915):24, 190, 192, 216, 219.

46. *Forerunner* 3 (July 1912):196; 4 (1913):140, 299, 336; 6 (October 1915):279.

47. *Forerunner* 2 (February 1911):58; 3 (October 1912):279.

48. *Forerunner* 6 (March 1915):83.

49. *Forerunner* 6 (July 1915):179. See also CPG in *Current History* 18 (August 1923):736: "The misused movement we call 'birth control' is intended to protect the mother from enforced childbearing, and has been most beneficial to the crowded poor. But in the present mishandling of that movement it has come to be, as it were, a free ticket for selfish and fruitless indulgence, and an aid in the lamentable misbehavior of our times."

50. *Forerunner* 3 (February 1912):54.

51. *Forerunner* 4 (February 1913):35. Key discussed her theoretical disagreement with CPG in the *Atlantic* 112 (July 1913):49–50.

52. O'Neill, *Everyone Was Brave*, 32.

53. *Forerunner* 2 (November 1911):288–91; 3 (September 1912):252; 4 (January 1913):6–7; 6 (November 1915):285–86.

54. *Forerunner* 7 (1916):214–15, 336.

55. *Forerunner* 1 (November 1910):8–10.

56. *Forerunner* 3 (February 1912):55; 6 (March 1915):73–74; *New York Times*, 17 November 1914, 9, col. 1.

57. Austin, *Earth Horizon*, 327.

58. *Forerunner* 5 (January 1915):26–27.

59. *Forerunner* 4 (November 1913):307.

60. *Forerunner* 7 (October 1916):270.

61. *Forerunner* 3 (July 1912):196.

62. *Forerunner* 4 (August 1913):214.

63. *Forerunner* 4 (August 1913):213–14; 5 (1914), 138, 250; *New York Times,* 24 April 1914, 6, col. 1.

64. *Forerunner* 5 (September 1914):250–51.

65. *Forerunner* 5 (December 1914):321; *New York Times,* 6 January 1915, 15, col. 5.

66. *New York Times,* 16 October 1920, 2, col. 3.

67. *Forerunner* 7 (July 1916):193–95.

68. *Forerunner* 7 (1916):27, 120, 145–46, 307.

69. Foreword to *L,* xxxi.

70. *New York Evening Mail,* 14 April 1914, folder 295, CPG Papers.

71. Austin, *Earth Horizon,* 326.

72. *Forerunner* 7 (February 1916):56.

73. *Forerunner* 7 (December 1916):326.

74. CPG to Howells, 17 October 1919, HU.

Chapter Five

1. *Buffalo Evening News,* 29 August 1919, 7, cols. 2–4.

2. Louis Sullivan, *The Autobiography of an Idea* (New York: Press of the American Institute of Architects, Inc., 1924), 324. See also Jane Jacobs, *The Death and Life of Great American Cities* (New York: Random House, 1961), 24–25.

3. *Cosmopolitan* 38 (December 1904):139.

4. *Independent,* 14 July 1904, 70, 72. CPG later twice summarized this article in the *Forerunner* 2 (April 1911):111–13; 7 (October 1916):260–62.

5. *Forerunner* 4 (April 1913):104; *Survey,* 30 August 1913, 671.

6. *Forerunner* 7 (October 1916):277; 7 (December 1916):332; 6 (December 1915):316.

7. *L,* 316–17. See also the *Forerunner* 6 (October 1915):261–63; and the *Forum* 70 (October 1923):1983–89.

8. CPG to Alice Stone Blackwell, 19 January 1923 and 24 October 1930, NAWSA, carton 12, LC.

9. *Forerunner* 4 (July 1913):174–76.

10. *Independent,* 25 September 1920, 395.

11. *Century* 102 (July 1921):361–366.

12. CPG to Blackwell, 9 June 1915, NAWSA, carton 12, LC. See also foreword to *L,* xviii.

13. Black, "Woman Who Saw It First," 41.

14. *North American Review* 224 (December 1927):629.

15. "Feminism and Social Progress," in *Problems of Civilization* (New York, 1929), 131.

16. "Toward Monogamy," in *Our Changing Morality,* ed. Freda Kirchwey (New York, 1930), 65.

17. Unless otherwise noted, all reviews of *HRH* cited in this paragraph may be located in folder 307, CPG Papers.

18. *Bookman*, 24 January 1924, p. 575.

19. Foreword to *L*, xvii.

20. *Literary Review*, 1 December 1923, 303.

21. Folder 126, CPG Papers.

22. Folder 17, CPG Papers.

23. *Current History* 27 (October 1927):10.

24. "Toward Monogamy," 59; *L*, 318.

25. "Parasitism and Civilized Vice," in *Woman's Coming of Age*, ed S. D. Schmalhausen and V. F. Calverton (New York, 1931), 125.

26. *New York Review of Books*, 17 April 1980, 11.

27. Patricia M. Spacks, *The Female Imagination* (New York, 1975), 208, 217–18.

28. Folder 308, CPG Papers.

29. Spacks, *The Female Imagination*, 217.

30. *Forerunner* 4 (March 1913)67; 4 (September 1913):252.

31. Folder 231, CPG Papers.

32. Introduction to *CPGR*, xxxiv.

33. CPG to Benjamin Huebsch, 1 March 1932, LC.

34. CPG to Blackwell, 24 October 1930, NAWSA, carton 12, LC.

35. CPG to Blackwell, 29 December 1930, NAWSA, carton 12, LC.

36. CPG to Blackwell, 28 July 1931, NAWSA, carton 12, LC.

37. CPG to Blackwell, 7 January 1928, NAWSA, carton 12, LC.

38. Folder 17, CPG Papers.

39. CPG to Blackwell, 11 January 1935, NAWSA, carton 12, LC.

40. CPG to Blackwell, 15 April 1934, NAWSA, carton 12, LC. CPG's memory is not exact. Whitman had actually written "No array of terms can say how much I am at peace about God and about death."

41. Howe, "Charlotte Perkins Gilman," 216. See also CPG's posthumously published essay "The Right to Die," *Forum* 94 (November 1935):297–300.

42. *Forerunner* 3 (May 1912):130.

43. *New York Times*, 20 August 1935, 44, cols. 2–4.

44. Folder 284, CPG Papers.

45. *New York Times*, 20 August 1935, 44, col. 3.

46. Catt to CPG, 28 May 1935, folder 149, CPG Papers.

47. Catt to Chamberlain, 19 July 1940, folder 156, CPG Papers.

48. *American Quarterly* 8 (Spring 1956):39.

49. CPG to Blackwell, 15 April 1934, NAWSA, carton 12, LC.

Selected Bibliography

PRIMARY SOURCES

"Applepieville." *Independent,* 25 September 1920, 365, 393–95.
"The Beauty of a Block." *Independent,* 14 July 1904, 67–72.
Concerning Children. Boston: Small, Maynard, 1900.
The Charlotte Perkins Gilman Reader. Edited, with introduction, by Ann J. Lane. New York: Pantheon, 1980.
The Crux. Forerunner 2 (1911). Reprint. New York: Charlton, 1911.
"Feminism and Social Progress." In *Problems of Civilization,* edited by Baker Brownell. New York: D. Van Nostrand, 1929, pp. 115–42.
Forerunner 1–7 (1909–16). Reprint. New York: Greenwood, 1968.
"The Giant Wistaria." *New England Magazine,* n.s. 4 (June 1891):480–85.
Herland. Forerunner 6 (1915), Reprint, with introduction by Ann J. Lane. New York: Pantheon, 1979.
His Religion and Hers: A Study of the Faith of Our Fathers and the Work of Our Mothers. New York: Century, 1923. Reprint. Westport, Conn.: Hyperion Press, 1976.
The Home: Its Work and Influence. New York: McClure, Phillips, 1903.
"How Home Conditions React Upon the Family." *American Journal of Sociology* 14 (March 1909):592–605.
Human Work. New York: McClure, Phillips, 1904.
In This Our World. Oakland: McCombs & Vaughn, 1893. 3d ed. Boston: Small, Maynard, 1898. Reprint. New York: Arno, 1974.
"Is America Too Hospitable?" *Forum,* 70 (October 1923):1983–89.
The Living of Charlotte Perkins Gilman: An Autobiography. With a foreword by Zona Gale. New York: Appleton-Century, 1935. Reprint. New York: Harper & Row, 1975.
"Making Towns Fit to Live In." *Century* 102 (July 1921):361–66.
The Man-Made World: Our Androcentric Culture. Forerunner 1 (1909–10). Reprint. New York: Charlton, 1911.
Moving the Mountain. Forerunner 2 (1911). Reprint. New York: Charlton, 1911.
"The Passing of the Home in Great American Cities." *Cosmopolitan* 38 (December 1904):137–47.

"Parasitism and Civilized Vice." In *Woman's Coming of Age,* edited by S. D. Schmalhausen. New York: Liveright, 1931, pp. 110–26.
"Progress through Birth Control." *North American Review* 224 (December 1927):622–29.
"Sex and Race Progress." In *Sex in Civilization,* edited by V. F. Calverton and S. D. Schmalhausen. New York: Macaulay, 1929, pp. 109–23.
"Social Darwinism." *American Journal of Sociology* 12 (March 1907):713–14.
"A Suggestion on the Negro Problem." *American Journal of Sociology* 14 (July 1908):78–85.
"Toward Monogamy." *Nation,* 11 June 1924, 671–73. Reprint. In *Our Changing Morality,* edited by Freda Kirchway. New York: Boni, 1930, pp. 53–66.
What Diantha Did. Forerunner 1 (1909–10), Reprint. New York: Charlton, 1910.
Women and Economics: A Study of the Economic Relation Between Men and Women as a Factor in Social Evolution. Boston: Small, Maynard, 1898. Reprint, with introduction by Carl Degler. New York: Harper & Row, 1966.
Women and Social Service. Warren, Ohio: National American Woman Suffrage Association, 1907.
"The Yellow Wall-paper." *New England Magazine* 5 (January 1892):647–59.

SECONDARY SOURCES

Bell, Millicent. "Pioneer." *New York Review of Books,* 17 April 1980, 10–14. An appreciative review of Hill's biography and, in its own right, an excellent overview of Gilman's life and major works.
Berkin, Carol. "Private Woman, Public Woman: The Contradictions of Charlotte Perkins Gilman." In *Women in America: A History.* Boston: Houghton Mifflin, 1979, pp. 150–73. Excellent introduction to Gilman's life and works. "Charlotte Perkins Gilman struggled for intellectual and emotional liberation, hampered through much of her life by an internalization of the very split vision of masculine and feminine spheres and destinies that, in her work, she would expose as artificial."
Black, Alexander. "The Woman Who Saw It First." *Century* 107 (November 1923):33–42. A perceptive summary of Gilman's career by a friend and contemporary.
Degler, Carl N. "Charlotte Perkins Gilman on the Theory and Practice of Feminism." *American Quarterly* 8 (Spring 1956):21–39. The article that inaugurated the modern revival of interest in Gilman. Especially valuable on *Women and Economics* and *The Man-Made World.*

Dell, Floyd. *Women as World Builders.* Chicago: Forbes, 1913, pp. 22–29. A favorable review of Gilman's literature by a prominent socialist writer, though marred by several inaccuracies.

Gale, Zona. "Charlotte Perkins Gilman." *Nation,* 25 September 1935, 350–51. A brief, eulogistic obituary by an eminent novelist.

Gilbert, Sandra, and Susan Gubar. *The Madwoman in the Attic: The Woman Writer and the Nineteenth-Century Imagination.* New Haven: Yale University Press, 1979, pp. 89–92. Excellent analysis of "The Yellow Wall-paper" as a "paradigmatic tale" of the plight of literary women.

Gornick, Vivian. "Twice-Told Tales." *Nation,* 23 September 1978, 278–81. Considers "The Yellow Wall-paper" a "metaphor for the fatal suffocation of spirit" that often afflicted nineteenth-century women.

Hayden, Dolores. "Charlotte Perkins Gilman and the Kitchenless House." *Radical History Review* 21 (Fall 1979):225–47. A first-rate analysis of Gilman's proposals for communities of kitchenless houses and apartment hotels.

Hedges, Elaine. Afterword to *The Yellow Wall-paper.* Old Westbury, N.Y.: Feminist Press, 1973, pp. 37–63. Pioneering study of Gilman's best story as a feminist document, though flawed by a tendency to consider it thinly disguised memoir.

Hill, Mary A. "Charlotte Perkins Gilman: A Feminist's Struggle with Womanhood." *Massachusetts Review* 21 (1980):503–26. Excellent introduction to Gilman's life and work. Examines the relationship of Gilman's early struggle, in particular, with her feminist convictions.

_____. *Charlotte Perkins Gilman: The Making of a Radical Feminist 1860–1896.* Philadelphia: Temple University Press, 1980. The major work of Gilman scholarship published to date. Extremely valuable delineation of Gilman's early difficulties, especially her adolescent trials. Less valuable and reliable treatments of her intellectual relationships and political associations. Occasionally, interpretations verge on guesswork.

Howe, Harriet. "Charlotte Perkins Gilman—As I Knew Her." *Equal Rights,* 5 September 1936, 211–16. Memoir by a feminist and close friend.

Hughes, James L. "Charlotte Perkins Gilman." *Canadian Magazine* 61 (August 1923):335–38. Brief reminiscence by a Gilman acquaintance.

Kennard, Jean K. "Convention Coverage or How to Read Your Own Life." *New Literary History* 13 (Autumn 1981):69–88. A phenomenological reading of "The Yellow Wall-paper," erroneously described at one point as a "novel." Relies upon feminist interpretations.

Kessler, Carol Farley. "Brittle Jars and Bitter Jangles: Light Verse by Charlotte Perkins Gilman." *Regionalism and the Female Imagination* 4 (1979):35–43. Examines some of Gilman's neglected early lyrics and concludes that her verses "have unquestionably radical intent."

Kolodny, Annette. "A Map for Rereading: Or, Gender and the Interpretation of Literary Texts." *New Literary History* 11 (Spring 1980):451–67, esp. 455–60. Accounts in general terms for the eclipse of "The Yellow Wall-paper" as a Poesque horror story and its emergence in the 1970s as a parable of the plight of married women in the nineteenth century.

MacPike, Loralee. "Environment as Psychopathological Symbolism in 'The Yellow Wallpaper.' " *American Literary Realism* 8 (Summer 1975):286–88. Reads "The Yellow Wall-paper" as an exercise in psychological realism.

Magner, Lois N. "Women and the Scientific Idiom: Textual Episodes from Wollstonecraft, Fuller, Gilman, and Firestone." *Signs* 4 (Autumn 1978):61–80, esp. 68–77. Discusses the metaphors Gilman derived from physics and biology. Flawed by a failure to distinguish between conservative or deterministic and reform Darwinism.

Nies, Judith. *Seven Women.* New York: Viking, 1977, pp. 127–45. An excellent biographical sketch, especially of Gilman's early years.

O'Neill, William L. *Everyone Was Brave.* New York: Quadrangle, 1969, pp. 38–44, 130–33. Summarizes Gilman's "scorching attack on the maternal pieties" in *Women and Economics* and *The Home.* Perceptive biographical sketch which notes the limitations of Gilman's thought.

Pearson, Carol. "Coming Home: Four Feminist Utopias and Patriarchal Experience." In *Future Females: A Critical Anthology.* Edited by Marleen S. Barr. Bowling Green, Ohio: Bowling Green State University Popular Press, 1981, pp. 63–70. Notes several points of consensus among four feminist utopian novels, including *Herland.*

Schöpp-Schilling, Beate. " 'The Yellow Wallpaper': A Rediscovered 'Realistic' Story." *American Literary Realism* 8 (Summer 1975):284–86. Discusses the symbolic significance of the nursery, the barred windows, the bedstead, and the wallpaper.

Scott, Anne Firor. "A New-Model Woman." *Review in American History* 8 (December 1980):442–47. Provocative review-essay of Hill's biography. Recommends that Gilman's career be considered in the broader context of the social movements in which she participated.

Spacks, Patricia Meyer. *The Female Imagination.* New York: Knopf, 1975, pp. 208–18. Analysis of Gilman's memoirs as "all superego and sickness."

Wellington, Amy. *Women Have Told: Studies in the Feminist Tradition.* Boston: Little, Brown, 1930, pp. 115–31. Excellent biographical sketch prepared with Gilman's cooperation.

Winkler, Barbara Scott. *Victorian Daughters: The Lives and Feminism of Charlotte Perkins Gilman and Olive Schreiner.* Occasional Paper in Women's Studies, no. 13, American Culture Program. Ann Arbor:

University of Michigan, 1980. Sound, if overwritten, intellectual-biographical sketch of Gilman. Draws largely upon her major essays.

Wood, Ann Douglas. " 'The Fashionable Diseases': Women's Complaints and Their Treatment in Nineteenth-Century America." *Journal of Interdisciplinary History* 4 (Summer 1973):25–52, esp. 41–44. Discusses Gilman's treatment for nervous prostration and her re-creation of the episode in "The Yellow Wall-paper" from the perspective of a social historian.

Index